He that believeth and is baptized shall be saved;
but he that believeth not shall be damned.
~ Jesus Christ (Mark 16:16 KJV)

THE
MYSTERY OF
WATER BAPTISM

Understanding Water Baptism

CHRISTOPHER OGAN

THE MYSTERY OF WATER BAPTISM

Copyright © 2019 Christopher Ogan

ISBN : 978-978-972-647-9

Published by The Living Word Media

Follow us on Facebook: @TheLivingWordDevotional

The ebook version of this book is available on Amazon.com

All scripture quotations are from the King James Version of the Holy Bible unless otherwise stated.

The portions of the scriptures made bold are highlighted to emphasise particular areas of interest in the scriptures.

DEDICATION

I dedicate this book to my beloved father, Elder Sylvanus Umari Ogan.

I also dedicate this book to all mankind whom God has ordained for salvation in Christ from the foundation of the world, who have not been baptised into Christ.

.

CONTENTS

PREFACE

Waiting for my turn to teach water baptism at a foundation class in a mega church and desperate for revelation to drive the truth into the heart of those who have just surrendered their life to Jesus, I could feel the Holy Spirit opening the seals to me, seal after seal, with such deep insights that I have never heard nor seen before.

This revelation from the Holy Spirit about water baptism is what I will be sharing with you in this book. This book is written by the wisdom of God for the salvation and blessing of all who have been ordained for salvation from the foundation of the world. It is written that men may know the truth that will make them free.

Preaching the gospel of Jesus and teaching men the mysteries of the Holy Bible has been a passion for me. I believe I have been fearfully and wonderfully designed and created for this purpose. Therefore expect a revelation that will illuminate your life as you read through the pages of this book.

Remain ever blessed.

Introduction:

If the foundations be destroyed, what can the righteous do?

~ Psalm 11:3.

One of the fundamental and foundational requirement for man's salvation and access to heaven is water baptism. The Lord Jesus made this clear after His resurrection when He said *"He that believeth and is baptised shall be saved* (Mark 16:16), also in John 3:5 He said emphatically that "*Except a man be born of water and of the Spirit, he cannot enter into the kingdom of God"*. From these eternal words of Christ we see that water baptism is necessary for man's salvation and access to heaven.

This all-important mystery however has been abused by those who do not truly understand its purpose and essence. Dr. Myles Munroe said, *"When purpose is not known, abuse is inevitable"*, this is exactly what has happened to water baptism. The purpose of water baptism has eluded many church leaders and as such it has suffered so much abuse and controversy in their hands. It is important to note however that no part of the Bible is controversial; it is the lack of scriptural understanding that makes people think it's controversial. Many believers (church leaders inclusive) do not understand what happens at baptism, neither do they understand its purpose and that is why they feel it is not necessary for salvation.

The need to truly understand water baptism especially in this dispensation of grace cannot be overemphasised. However to understand this mystery we must approach it from its foundation. This is because to get it right in anything, it must first be gotten right from the foundation.

Until the foundation of a matter is gotten right, whatever is done upon the faulty foundation is done in futility. As seen in Psalm 11:3 "*If the foundation be destroyed, what can the righteous do?*". In other words if the foundation of a religious practice or ordinance is destroyed, faulty, shaky or unstable there is nothing the righteous can do to salvage the situation, unless of course the foundation is fixed.

A faulty foundation is a risky ground to stand on. A faulty foundation puts everyone standing on it at risk of being destroyed. Anything or anyone resting on a faulty or shaky foundation is at risk of being destroyed. If the foundation of an important ordinance like water baptism is not gotten right, every believer resting on the faulty foundation is at risk of being destroyed. One striking thing about foundation is that, it determines the fate of whatever rests upon it.

Its important to note that, if the foundation of an ordinance is faulty, it can invalidate that ordinance, it is therefore vital to get the foundation of any ordinance right, if we must enjoy the blessings of that ordinance. Water baptism is a spiritual ordinance ordained by God for the spiritual rebirth of His children, therefore an understanding of the foundation of this ordinance is vital for all believers.

Drawing inspirations from the words of God in Psalm 82:5, we see that lack of knowledge and understanding about any spiritual mystery or ordinance can affect the foundation of that ordinance.

Psalm 82:5. They know not, neither will they understand; they walk on in darkness: all the foundations of the earth are out of course.

It's more like saying, as a result of man's lack of knowledge and understanding, the foundations of the earth have gone out of course.

A good knowledge and understanding of an ordinance is not only important in sustaining the foundation of that ordinance but it is also important in securing the blessings of that ordinance.

In this book we would be looking at water baptism

from its very foundation. From scriptures, we see that the teachings of Jesus Christ, the apostles and the prophets are our solid foundation (Ephesians 2:20), therefore any teaching, principle or ordinance that does not align with this foundational teachings must be taken with a pinch of salt, including any that may be found in this book.

In the light of the above, the mystery of water baptism in this book will be built upon the foundational teachings of Jesus Christ, the apostles and the prophets, with the teachings of Jesus Christ being the chief cornerstone. Through this book inspired by the Holy Spirit we will see what happens at water baptism and understand its purpose and benefits as documented in the Holy Scriptures.

My earnest desire and prayer is that your eyes of understanding will be opened to the mystery of water baptism as you read through the pages of this highly inspired book.

What Is Water Baptism?

To understand the term water baptism its important to take a look at the origin of the word "Baptism". Baptism is derived from the Greek word "βαπτιζω", which in English letters is translated as *"baptizō"*. The Greek word *"baptizō"* literally means to "dip" or to "immerse".

Water baptism in simple term could therefore mean to dip or immerse in water. The essence of water baptism however has been expressed using various terms based on the perspective of the author. Apostle Titus for instance saw water baptism as the washing of regeneration (Titus 3:5).

From my perspective and to stick to the basics, *I*

see water baptism as an ordinance ordained by God for the spiritual rebirth of the repentant soul. It is a medium through which the repentant soul who believes in the Lord Jesus identifies with His death and resurrection, by being immersed in water in the name of the Father and the Son and the Holy Spirit, thus being united with Him in Spirit and in truth.

Scriptural references:

> *Matthew 28:19. Go ye therefore, and teach all nations,* **baptizing them in the name of the Father, and of the Son, and of the Holy Ghost:**

> *Acts 2:38. Then Peter said unto them,* **Repent, and be baptized** *every one of you in the name of Jesus Christ for the remission of sins,* **and ye shall receive the gift of the Holy Ghost.**

> *Mark 16:16.* **He that believeth and is baptized shall be saved***; but he that believeth not shall be damned.*

> *Romans 6:3. Know ye not, that so many of us as were* **baptized into Jesus Christ** *were* **baptized into his death?**

IMPORTANT POINTS TO NOTE ABOUT WATER BAPTISM

#1: WATER BATISM IS A COMMANDMENT AND AN INTEGRAL PART OF THE GREAT COMMISSION.

A commandment is something that is commanded and we see from scriptures that water baptism is a commandment that must be obeyed. The great commission does not only involve preaching the gospel, it includes water baptism. Water baptism is an integral part of the great commission. Preaching the gospel and not baptising those that believe in the gospel is not a fulfilment of the great commission.

> *Matthew 28:18. And Jesus came and spake unto them, saying, All power is given unto me in heaven and in earth.*
> *19. Go ye therefore, and* **teach all nations, baptizing them** *in the name of the Father, and of the Son, and of the Holy Ghost:*
> *20.* **Teaching them to observe all things** *whatsoever I have* **commanded** *you: and, lo, I am with you alway, even unto the end of the world. Amen.*
>
> *Mark 16:15. And he said unto them,* **Go ye into all the world, and preach the gospel to every**

creature.

*16. **He that believeth and is baptized shall be saved**; but he that believeth not shall be damned.*

*19. So then **after the Lord had spoken unto them, he was received up into heaven, and sat on the right hand of God.***

The Lord Jesus Christ after His resurrection commanded his disciples to teach and baptise men from all nations of the earth. These words were among the last words the Lord Jesus said before He ascended into heaven to sit on the right hand of God. Jesus is sitting on the right hand of God looking upon the earth to see those that will obey the commandment of the great commission for Him to confirm His word and the purpose of water baptism in their life.

To reflect the importance of this commandment, it was given after the blood sacrifice of Jesus Christ and after the resurrection when the Lord Jesus had received all power in Heaven and in Earth. If the death and resurrection of Christ nullified water baptism the Lord Jesus would not have made it a fundamental requirement for the salvation of men, when He announced the great commission after His death on the cross. So the death and resurrection of Christ does not do away with water baptism or make water baptism irrelevant is the dispensation of grace. It is rather an essential and fundamental requirement for our access to grace. As a matter of truth we need water baptism even more in this dispensation of grace.

From scriptures we see that through baptism we identify with what Christ did for us at Calvary, in other words to benefit from the death and resurrection of Christ and all that it brings (grace inclusive) we must be baptised into Him. We can only partake of the benefits of redemption (power, riches, wisdom, strength, honour, glory, blessing) after we get baptised in water, because it is at baptism that we identify with the death and resurrection of Christ, it is at baptism that we identify with what Christ did for us at Calvary.

#2: WATER BAPTISM IS A FUNDAMENTAL REQUIREMENT FOR THE SALVATION OF MEN.

We see from scriptures that water baptism is necessary for the salvation of men. It is a prerequisite for man's salvation. The Lord Jesus made it clear after His resurrection.

> *Mark 16:16. He that believeth **and is baptized shall be saved**; but he that believeth not shall be damned.*

The idea that water baptism is not necessary for salvation is a lie of the devil to hinder many from being saved. Since Jesus Christ was crucified and the devil saw that he had failed by sponsoring His crucifixion, he has not given up on trying to hinder the ministry of Jesus. And one of such ways the devil tries to hinder the salvation ministry of Jesus Christ is to remove water baptism (such a fundamental requirement for man's salvation) from the equation. Jesus said **He that believeth and is baptized shall be saved**, to remove baptism from that statement turns it to a half-truth and half-truth as we know is as deceitful and deadly as a lie. If the Lord Jesus had fallen for the half truth the devil tried to sell to him in the wilderness, I wonder what would have happened to mankind, but thank God He knew the other half of the truth, and He said, *thou shall not tempt the Lord thy God* (Luke 4:10-12). If you still believe that water baptism is not necessary for salvation, you believe a lie of the devil and that lie can hinder you from being saved.

From the statement of Jesus in Mark 16:16, we must understand that water baptism has the same potency to connect us to our salvation in Christ as much as faith has. Water baptism is as important as faith is for man's salvation.

Apostle Peter reveals to us how that water baptism is necessary for the salvation of our soul. He reveals to us how that water has been a tool for the salvation of men since the time of Noah, and still remains an effective tool for the salvation of men today, in the form of water baptism.

*1 Peter 3:20. Which sometime were disobedient, when once the longsuffering of God waited in the days of Noah, while the ark was a preparing, wherein few, that is, **eight souls were saved by water.***

*21. The like figure whereunto even **baptism doth also now save us** (not the putting away of the filth of the flesh, but the answer of a good conscience toward God,) by the resurrection of Jesus Christ:*

*Baptism **now** saves us by the resurrection of Christ.*
I like the way the New Living Translation puts the above scripture.

*1 Peter 3:21 (NLT). And **that water is a picture of baptism**, which now saves you, not by removing dirt from your body, but as a response to God from a clean conscience. **It is effective because of the resurrection of Jesus Christ.***

Water baptism is effective because of the resurrection of Jesus Christ. The resurrection of Christ empowers water baptism to save us. The resurrection of Christ does not nullify water baptism rather it makes it an effective tool for man's salvation. *Water baptism draws its power and potency to save from the resurrection of Christ.* Water baptism is powered by the death and resurrection of Christ. If by dipping himself seven times in water Naaman's skin became like that of a child (2 Kings 5:14) even when the resurrection of Christ was not involved, then imagine what water baptism could do for us, now that it is empowered and powered by the resurrection of Christ.

We also see from the scripture that water baptism is a response to God's call for repentance in other to have a good conscience towards God. We respond to God's call for repentance by getting baptised, no wonder Apostle Peter would always say *"Repent and be baptised"*. We show repentance by getting baptised and that is where salvation begins. We see how that water baptism is a fundamental requirement for the salvation of men.

#3: WATER BAPTISM IS A DEMONSTRATION OF OUR FAITH IN CHRIST, IT VALIDATES OR GIVES LIFE TO OUR FAITH.

> *James 2:14. What doth it profit, my brethren, though a man say he hath faith, and have not works? can faith save him?*
> *17. Even so **faith, if it hath not works, is dead, being alone**.*
> *18. Yea, a man may say, Thou hast faith, and I have works: shew me thy faith without thy works, and **I will shew thee my faith by my***

works.

19. Thou believest that there is one God; thou doest well: the devils also believe, and tremble.

*20. But wilt thou know, O vain man, that **faith without works is dead?***

21. Was not Abraham our father justified by works, when he had offered Isaac his son upon the altar?

*22. Seest thou how faith wrought with his works, and **by works was faith made perfect?***

*24. Ye see then how that **by works a man is justified**, and not by faith only.*

*26. For **as the body without the spirit is dead, so faith without works is dead also.***

Water baptism is a demonstration of our faith in Christ, it is an act of faith and obedience to the commands of God. Understanding water baptism as a demonstration of our faith in Christ is the *missing link* that has made many to misunderstand the true purpose of water baptism. When we see water baptism as an act of faith, it becomes easy to understand the purpose and essence of water baptism. Believing in Christ and being baptised go hand in hand. Our faith in Christ is not valid without water baptism because our faith in Christ is demonstrated through baptism.

From the above scriptures we can see the following...

- *Faith without works cannot save a man.*
- *Faith cannot survive alone without works.*
- *Faith needs works to be alive.*
- *Faith needs work to work.*
- *Faith without works is dead.*
- *Faith is expressed through works.*
- *Faith without works does not make your faith any different from the devil's.*
- *Faith is made perfect by works.*
- *A man is justified by his works.*
- *Works justifies man.*

The works spoken of by apostle James simply refers to deeds or actions, I prefer to refer to this works as ***the works of faith***. In this light I would like to simply define works in this context as the demonstration of faith or taking steps of faith in obedience to God's word, instruction or command. God gave father Abraham an instruction and he obeyed and that action justified him as the father of faith. When we say we have faith in Christ there is what to do to prove that we truly believe. Note therefore that water baptism is the corresponding action that demonstrate, expresses, proves or validates our faith in Christ. To believe in Christ and not show or express it in our action would make our faith vain.

Drawing inspiration from James 2:26, we see also that our faith must be accompanied by an action to truly be alive, for any faith without a corresponding action is a dead and worthless faith. Going by what is written in the book of James as seen above, if faith is a body and works (deeds) is a spirit, I would say *water baptism is the spirit of our faith in Christ*, in otherwords water baptism gives life to our faith in Christ. We see therefore that water baptism is a deed that we must do (or an action we must take) to give life to our faith in Christ and that without water baptism our faith in Christ would be dead and invalid.

Also as seen in James 2:26, we must understand that faith is not just a mental or cognitive perception but also a visible physical or practical action. Our cognitive perception of faith most often must be expressed and validated by a visible work or action. Faith cannot be seen but it's action can be seen, that is why we are told to look out for the actions, deeds or signs of faith, the Lord Jesus said in Mark 16:17, *And this signs shall follow them that believe*, in otherwords if you want to know those that believe, look out for their signs or deeds. He also said *by their fruits (deeds/actions) ye shall know them*, we see therefore that it takes what we do to know what is inside of us, it takes our actions of faith to know if we truly have faith.

I see also that works does not only give life to faith but it is also the proof of the presence of faith. Faith may be an invisible force but it can be seen in our actions. We don't see when a spirit leaves a man's body at death but we know for sure that a man is dead when he becomes inactive for a while. The absence of works (action of faith) is the visible proof of a dead faith, just as the absence of the spirit in a body or the inactivity of the body is a proof of death. We see therefore that **works does not only give life to our faith but it is also the proof of a living faith.**

We must understand that our faith in Christ and water baptism are like body and spirit, you must not separate the two, when the two are separated one dies and that which dies is faith. The Lord Jesus Christ shows us this body and spirit relationship in Mark 16:16 when He said *He that believeth and is baptized shall be saved.* Believe here is the body while baptism is the spirit.

From Mark 16:16, we see faith (as a body) and water baptism (its spirit) side by side. This duo, faith in Christ and baptism must not be separated if our faith in Christ must be kept alive. Just as a man's spirit must not be separated from his body if he must stay alive, in the same manner to keep our faith in Christ alive we must be baptised in water. Baptism makes our faith in Christ alive and active, without water baptism our faith in Christ is inactive. *Faith in Christ without water baptism is a potential faith; faith in Christ plus water baptism is a kinetic and dynamic faith*. A potential faith is inactive and non productive while a kinetic faith is active and productive. It's important to note that a potential faith does not change anything neither is God moved by a potential faith; it takes a kinetic and dynamic faith to move God to save and transform us.

We have seen that water baptism validates our faith in Christ and is a living proof of our faith in the finished work of Jesus Christ; without submitting ourselves to be baptised our faith becomes vain and invalid. Please know that you are not a believer until you do what you believe, because your action validates your faith.

I must say at this point that many so-called believers in Christ who are not baptised in water are not believers because they do not validate their faith by doing what they believe. If you believe in Christ and you are not baptised in water, you are not yet a believer in Christ, because you have not identified with the death and resurrection of Christ. You can however validate your faith today by getting baptised in water.

The Ethiopian eunuch excitedly validated his faith by being baptised in water.

> *Acts 8:36. And as they went on their way, they came unto a certain water: and the eunuch said, **See, here is water; what doth hinder me to be baptized?***
>
> *37. And Philip said, **If thou believest with all thine heart, thou mayest**. And he answered and said, I believe that Jesus Christ is the Son of God.*
>
> *38. And he commanded the chariot to stand still: and they went down both into the water,*

*both Philip and the eunuch; and he baptized
him.*

If you believe in Jesus Christ, you will show or act it by being baptised in water.

From Apostle Philip's response to the eunuch in the above scripture we see that **the only condition for water baptism is our absolute faith in Christ**. In other words after we have believed in Christ, we don't need to go through months of baptismal teachings or classes before we get baptised because if we die within that period of delay before baptism, we may not be saved.

#4: WATER BAPTISM REQUIRES FAITH IN
      CHRIST TO BE VALID.

It's important to note that water baptism without faith in Christ will simply result in a body bath. Faith in Christ is a requirement for the New Testament water baptism to be effective or valid.

> *Acts 8:36. And as they went on their way, they came unto a certain water: and the eunuch said,* **See, here is water; what doth hinder me to be baptized?**
> *37. And Philip said,* **If thou believest with all thine heart, thou mayest.** *And he answered and said, I believe that Jesus Christ is the Son of God.*

If thou believest with all thine heart, thou mayest.

In otherwords, if you do not believe in Christ with all your heart, you may not get baptised.

The above statement by Philip reveals to us how that our absolute faith in Christ is required, for water baptism to be effective or valid. We see a classical example of how that faith in Christ is necessary for baptism, in the ministry of Philip.

Acts 8:12. But **when they believed Philip preaching** *the things* **concerning the kingdom of God, and the name of Jesus Christ, they were baptized,** *both men and women.*

The people of Samaria got baptised when they believed in Jesus Christ. Only those that believed in Christ were baptised in the early church. The same should apply today, such that only those that believe in Jesus Christ should be baptised.

The Lord Jesus in Mark 16:16 confirms the necessity of faith for water baptism when He said; *He that believeth and is baptised shall be saved.* Obviously, absolute faith in Christ is a necessary requirement for water baptism.

If faith in Christ is required for water baptism to be valid, then infant baptism is invalid, because an infant is incapable of believing. It therefore seems obvious that a child should be baptised only when they have attained an age when they know right from wrong (according to God's word) and can believe in the gospel and in Jesus Christ. We therefore, see how that water baptism without faith in Christ is simply a body bath.

#5: WATER BAPTISM IS A REQUIREMENT TO ENTER HEAVEN.

> *Mark 16:15. And he said unto them, Go ye into all the world, and preach the gospel to every creature.*
> *16. He that believeth and is baptized shall be saved; but he that believeth not shall be damned.*

The Lord Jesus Christ said, *He that believes AND is baptized shall be saved and he that believeth not shall be damned.* Note that the Bible did not say he that believeth only, you have to believe and also be baptised. In other words, if you only believe you can't be saved, you must be baptised also to be saved.

You know, many believers get confused when they read the statement *...but he that believeth not shall be damned,* observing that baptism was not mentioned in the second statement made by the Lord Jesus.

However, when we see water baptism as a demonstration of faith it becomes easy to understand this statement, because when we have faith in Christ, it is expected that we will demonstrate or show it by getting baptised. From the above scripture it is expected that he that believes in Christ will demonstrate his faith by getting baptised, it was therefore not necessary to add baptism wherever believe appears. It's important to note that wherever believe is seen in scriptures, there is always what to do to demonstrate what we believe.

Without getting baptised, you are not a candidate for heaven. The Lord Jesus in John 3:5, made it clear with all emphasis that *"Except a man be born of water, he cannot enter into the kingdom of God"*. Literally this scripture emphasises the importance of water baptism. We see therefore that water baptism is a spiritual rebirth that prepares us for heaven. Those who say baptism is not necessary for salvation or necessary to enter heaven are indirectly depriving those who do not get baptised (due to this lack of knowledge) the opportunity to enter heaven, it becomes unto them like the Lord Jesus said in Luke 11 verse 52, *Woe unto you, lawyers! for ye have taken away the key of knowledge: ye entered not in yourselves, and them that were entering in ye hindered.*

Someone may ask, if we must be baptised to enter heaven, then it means those who were on earth before Christ came to earth would not enter heaven because they were not baptised.

The truth is that they were baptised in water at one point or the other, every member of the church in the wilderness were baptised when they went through the Red Sea and other seas.

> *1 Corinthians 10:2. And were all baptized unto Moses in the cloud and in the sea;*

Now, note that to complete the immersion from head to toe, they were baptised in the sea and were also baptised in the cloud through rain. The sea baptises them from their toe upwards while the cloud baptised them from the crown of their head downwards to complete the baptism. The baptism was part of the reason they went through the Red Sea and other seas. The mystery of water baptism is an ancient mystery that even when man did not know, understand or is conscious of it, yet God still used it to prepare the people for their promised land and for heaven. Even though water baptism was only known or revealed to man during the time of John the Baptist yet it had been an ancient secret mystery, which only God knew.

This mystery was revealed at the time of John to help us do all the words of God. We see from the Holy Scriptures that the things which are revealed to us are revealed to enable us do what God has commanded.

> *Deuteronomy 29:29. The secret things belong unto the LORD our God: but* ***those things which are revealed belong unto us*** *and to our children for ever,* ***that we may do all the words of this law.***

The mystery of water baptism was revealed to us to help, empower and enable us to do what God commands us. We see the Lord Jesus attest to this truth when He said in Matthew 3:15 that baptism was necessary for us to do the will of God.

We see therefore that water baptism is an ancient mystery ordained by God and practised by God Himself. So those in the Old Testament were baptised with the baptism of the cloud and sea in preparation for heaven.

A lack of knowledge of the truth about water baptism will shut the door of heaven to many. You know many people use the example of the repentant criminal on the cross to justify why water baptism is not necessary to enter heaven. However, if we see water baptism as a medium that empowers us to do the will of God as the Lord Jesus revealed in Matthew 3:15, it becomes easy to understand that **if you are not** in a near death situation you will need water baptism in other to do God's will while you are alive. Interestingly, majority of the people who hear the gospel are not in a near death situation, therefore a near death situation should not be an example to those who are full of life. A near death situation should not be used to justify what should happen in a full life situation, just as the approach used to save a patient at near death does not apply to a patient full of life. Also from the insight in 1 Corinthians 10 verse 2, have you ever thought that the repentant criminal could have been baptised in the cloud unto Jesus. God could have made it rain that day just to get this repentant soul baptised. Well, on a final note, unlike the dying man at the cross, if you do not die or are not dying at the point of confessing Jesus as your Lord and Saviour, then you must ensure that you get baptised.

#6: WATER BAPTISM IS THE WASHING OF
   REGENERATION.

Our new life in Christ begins at baptism. Apostle Titus calls baptism the washing of regeneration.

> *Titus 3:5. Not by works of righteousness which we have done, but according to his mercy he saved us, by the washing of regeneration, and renewing of the Holy Ghost;*

Regeneration is synonymous with rebirth or new birth. We see therefore that our new birth experience actually begins at baptism, no wonder the Lord Jesus in John 3:5 says we must be born of water. We would look at this in detail in the next chapter.

#7: WATER BAPTISM IS THE BODY BEING BORN AGAIN.

Drawing inspiration from Apostle Titus above we see that water baptism is the washing of regeneration or spiritual rebirth. Regeneration means renewal, rebirth or new birth. Also looking at water baptism as a spiritual circumcision (Colossians 2:11), we see that the circumcision of the flesh is like a rebirth process, that removes every coat of sin and hardness of the flesh, more like what happened to Naaman in 2 Kings 5:14 where his skin became like that of a little child when he dipped himself in water. I believe the same happens when we get baptised though in a way that is not visible to the natural eye, as apostle Paul rightly calls it, *a circumcision made without hands*. When we are baptised something happens to our body (a spiritual circumcision) that is not visible to the natural eyes. That experience is what I refer to as the body being born again.

You know before now many people think that when we get born again only our spirit is involved, that only our spirit gets born again but that is not true, our body can also get born again. Note that the Lord Jesus in John 3:5 presented to us two media (water and Spirit) for our spiritual rebirth: which I believe the water is for our body (flesh) and the Spirit is for our spirit. We see therefore that our body gets born again by water while our spirit gets born again by the Holy Spirit.

John 3:5. Jesus answered, Verily, verily, I say unto thee, Except a man be born of water and of the Spirit, he cannot enter into the kingdom of God.
6. That which is born of the flesh is flesh; and that which is born of the Spirit is spirit.

"For that which is born of the Spirit is spirit", that is to say that which gets born or transformed by the Holy Spirit is our spirit.

"That which is born of the flesh is flesh", talking about natural birth, that is, that which is given birth to by the flesh (as seen in physical child birth) is flesh, and that flesh remains flesh and continues to fulfil the lust and desires of the flesh except it becomes reborn through water baptism, so YES! Your body can get born again, Hallelujah! Please hear this, your flesh needs to be circumcised or reborn through water baptism, otherwise it would continue to manifest what it knows best - carnality or the works of the flesh, which is sin. You need water baptism to be able to put your body under subjection. For your body to become holy even by the help of the Holy Spirit you need to be baptised in water, because an unbaptized flesh cannot overcome sin. An unbaptized flesh is not sensitive to the leading of the Holy Spirit, which makes it impossible to walk in the Spirit, put the body under subjection and overcome sin. Dearly beloved, your body must be born again of water through baptism to be able to overcome sin.

#8: WATER BAPTISM IS THE NEXT THING WE MUST DO AFTER WE SURRENDER TO JESUS AND CONFESS HIM AS OUR LORD.

When Saul encountered the Lord Jesus, the Lord told Saul that he would be told what to do by a man named Ananias. And we see from scriptures that the first thing Ananias told Saul to do was to get baptised. In other words we see the Lord Jesus indirectly recommending water baptism to Saul through His servant Ananias.

> *Acts 22:8. And I answered, Who art thou, Lord? And he said unto me, I am Jesus of Nazareth, whom thou persecutest.*
> *10. And I said, What shall I do, Lord? And the Lord said unto me, Arise, and go into Damascus; and **there it shall be told thee of all things which are appointed for thee to do.***
> *11. And when I could not see for the glory of that light, being led by the hand of them that were with me, I came into Damascus.*
> *12. And one Ananias, a devout man according to the law, having a good report of all the Jews which dwelt there,*
> *13. Came unto me, and stood, and said unto*

me, Brother Saul, receive thy sight. And the same hour I looked up upon him.

14. And he said, The God of our fathers hath chosen thee, that thou shouldest know his will, and see that Just One, and shouldest hear the voice of his mouth.

15. For thou shalt be his witness unto all men of what thou hast seen and heard.

16. And now why tarriest thou? **arise, and be baptized,** *and wash away thy sins, calling on the name of the Lord.*

Note that when Saul surrendered his life to Jesus and confessed Him as Lord, the next thing he did (or was told to do) was to get baptised. We see therefore that after we surrender to the Lord Jesus and confess Him as our Lord and Saviour (or go for altar call), the next thing we must do, is to IMMEDIATELY (or at the slightest opportunity) get baptised in water. The urgency in the need to get baptised in water after we surrender to Jesus as our Lord is seen in the words of Ananias *"Why tarriest thou?"* in verse 16 above.

The story of the Ethiopian eunuch in Acts 8:36-38 also corroborates this truth.

Water Baptism & New Birth

*John 3:3. Jesus answered and said unto him, Verily, verily, I say unto thee, **Except a man be born again**, he cannot see the kingdom of God.*
*5. Jesus answered, Verily, verily, I say unto thee, **Except a man be born of water and of the Spirit**, he cannot enter into the kingdom of God.*

You know many times we need to ask God questions in other to get answers to things we do not understand. Nicodemus asked the Lord Jesus a question about being born again that made Jesus to explain further what He meant to be born again. If Nicodemus had not asked the question, perhaps we would still be in confusion (like he was) concerning what it meant to be born again. Perhaps we wouldn't have known that it takes two mediums (water and Spirit) to become born again. I strongly believe that if Nicodemus had asked for more clarification of what it meant to be born of water, Jesus would have told him that he meant water baptism, because with all the overwhelming scriptural proofs and divine inspirations, I have no doubt that the Lord Jesus was referring to water baptism when He said *"be born of water"*.

As seen from scriptures, it's important to note that we get born again of water through water baptism. You cannot have the new creature experience written in 2 Corinthians 5:17 without water baptism.

At baptism we see the Godhead working together to bring about the birth of a new creature.

> *Mark 1:9. And it came to pass in those days, that Jesus came from Nazareth of Galilee, and was baptized of John in Jordan.*
> *10. And straightway coming up out of the water, he saw the heavens opened, and the* ***Spirit like a dove descending upon him:***
> *11. And there came* ***a voice from heaven****, saying,* ***Thou art my beloved Son****, in whom I am well pleased.*

From the above scripture we see the visible union of the Godhead working together. It's important to note that the appearance of the Godhead together always brings about the birth of a new thing. In Genesis chapter one verses two and three, we see the Godhead visibly working together and the result of that collaboration is the birth of the heaven and the earth and everything in it. We see the Holy Spirit moving upon the waters in verse two, and God the Father in verse three speaking Jesus, the Living Word and the Light of the world into being (John 1:1-5,14; John 8:12).

Just as the union of the Godhead in Genesis gave birth to a new thing, the visible union of the Godhead at the baptism of Jesus gave birth to a new Jesus. No wonder as Jesus was being baptised God said to Him, *"Thou art my beloved Son, in whom I am well pleased"*.

Now permit me to show you something of utmost importance to help us understand this mystery. First I would like to show you this word *"Thou art my beloved Son, in whom I am well pleased"* in prophecy. By prophecy I mean a prediction (statement made of what will happen in the future) made under divine inspiration. The word in prophecy is seen in Psalm two verse seven, where Jesus was speaking about Himself through David concerning what God said to Him.

*Psalm 2:7. I will declare the decree: the LORD hath said unto me, Thou art my Son; **this day have I begotten thee.***
The LORD hath said unto me…
Note that the capitalisation of the words of scripture

is used to identify the spiritual level of a being. This is often used for words that can be used to identify both God and man. When using the term *"lord"* LORD is used to identify God the Almighty Father, Lord is used to identify Jesus the Son of God and lord is used to identify man.

Keep this words in mind *"Thou art my Son;* ***this day have I begotten thee"***, especially the boldfaced words.

Note that the entire chapter two of the book of Psalm is speaking about Jesus Christ, Jesus Himself was the one speaking about Himself through king David. We must understand that most of the words written in the book of Psalm were not the words of David, some words were the direct words of Jesus Christ and the Holy Spirit speaking through king David (Acts 1:16).

Let's hear it from the author of the book of Psalms himself, king David.

2 Samuel 23:1. (KJV). Now these be the last words of David. David the son of Jesse said, and the man who was raised up on high, the anointed of the God of Jacob, and the sweet psalmist of Israel said,
2. ***The Spirit of the LORD spake by me***, *and his word was in my tongue.*

Many words spoken by Jesus and the Holy Ghost through David in the book of Psalms are prophecies concerning things that should happen in the future as seen in Acts 1:16-20 concerning Judas Iscariot.

Acts 1:16. Men and brethren, this scripture must needs have been fulfilled, **which the Holy Ghost by the mouth of David spake** *before concerning Judas, which was guide to them that took Jesus. 20. For it is written in the book of Psalms, Let his habitation be desolate, and let no man dwell therein: and his bishoprick let another take.*

We see therefore that the prophetic words of Jesus through king David in Psalm 2:7 was what was fulfilled in Mark 1:11, when Jesus was getting baptised. The account of apostle Paul below corroborates this truth that the above words in Psalm 2:7 were spoken concerning Jesus.

Acts 13:33. **God hath fulfilled** *the same unto us their children, in that he hath raised up Jesus again; as it is also* **written in the second psalm,** **Thou art my Son, this day have I begotten thee.**

Hebrews 5:5. So also Christ glorified not himself to be made an high priest; but he that said unto him, **Thou art my Son, to day have I begotten thee.**

Also note that the word Son in all the reference

scriptures above is written with a capital "S" signifying that it is referring to Jesus the Son of God.

To buttress the point that the words spoken by God when Jesus was getting baptised was in fulfilment to the word spoken in Psalm 2:7 and that most words spoken in the book of Psalm were not David's words but the direct words of Jesus Christ and the Holy Ghost, let's take a look at some of the prophesies made by Jesus and the Holy Ghost in the book of Psalm through David and their fulfilment in the New Testament.

PROPHECY: (JESUS SPEAKING)

Psalm 22: 1. **MY GOD, MY GOD, WHY HAST THOU FORSAKEN ME?** *why art thou so far from helping me, and from the words of my roaring?*
16. For dogs have compassed me: the assembly of the wicked have inclosed me: **they pierced my hands and my feet.**
18. **They part my garments among them, and cast lots upon my vesture.**

FULFILMENT:

For Verse 1
Matthew 27:46. And about the ninth hour Jesus cried with a loud voice, saying, Eli, Eli, lama sabachthani? that is to say, **My God, my God, why hast thou forsaken me?**

48. And straightway one of them ran, and took a spunge, and filled it with vinegar, and put it on a reed, and gave him to drink.

For Verses 16&18
*Matthew 27: 35. And they **crucified him, and parted his garments, casting lots: that it might be fulfilled which was spoken by the prophet**, They parted my garments among them, and upon my vesture did they cast lots.*

PROPHECY: (JESUS SPEAKING)

*Psalm 22:16. For dogs have compassed me: the assembly of the wicked have inclosed me: **they pierced my hands and my feet.***
*17. I may tell all my bones: **they look and stare upon me.***

FULFILMENT:

*John 19:37. And again another scripture saith, **They shall look on him whom they pierced.***

PROPHECY: (JESUS SPEAKING)

*Psalm 41: 9. Yea, **mine own familiar friend**, in whom I trusted, **which did eat of my bread, hath lifted up his*** *heel against me.*

FULFILMENT:
Matthew 26: 23. And he answered and said, **He that dippeth his hand with me in the dish, the same shall betray me.**
25. Then Judas, which betrayed him, answered and said, Master, is it I? He said unto him, Thou hast said.

PROPHECY: (JESUS SPEAKING)

Psalm 69: 9. For **the zeal of thine house hath eaten me up***; and the reproaches of them that reproached thee are fallen upon me.*
21. They gave me also gall for my meat; and **in my thirst they gave me vinegar to drink.**

FULFILMENT:

For Verse 9...
John 2: 16. And said unto them that sold doves, Take these things hence; make not my Father's house an house of merchandise.
17. And his disciples remembered that **it was written, The zeal of thine house hath eaten me up.**

For Verse 21...
John 19: 28. After this, Jesus knowing that all things were now accomplished, **that the scripture might be**

fulfilled, saith, I thirst.
29. Now there was set a vessel full of vinegar: **and they**
filled a spunge with vinegar, and put it upon hyssop,
and put it to his mouth.

PROPHECY: (JESUS SPEAKING)

Psalm 2: 7. I will declare the decree: the LORD hath
said unto me, **Thou art my Son; this day have I**
begotten thee.

Psalm 16: 10. For thou wilt not leave my soul in hell;
neither wilt thou suffer thine Holy One to see
corruption.

FULFILMENT:

1st scripture...

Acts 13:33. **God hath fulfilled the same** *unto us their*
children, in that he hath raised up Jesus again; as it is
also written in the second psalm, **Thou art my Son, this**
day have I begotten thee.

2nd scripture...

Acts 13:35. Wherefore he saith also in another psalm,
Thou shalt not suffer thine Holy One to see
corruption.

PROPHECY: (HOLY SPIRIT SPEAKING)

Psalm 69:25. **Let their habitation be desolate***; and* **let none dwell in their tents.**
26. For they persecute him whom thou hast smitten; and they talk to the grief of those whom thou hast wounded.
27. Add iniquity unto their iniquity: and let them not come into thy righteousness.
28. **Let them be blotted out of the book of the living, and not be written with the righteous.**

Psalm 109: 6. Set thou a wicked man over him: and **let Satan stand at his right hand.**
8. Let his days be few; and **let another take his office.**
9. Let his children be fatherless, and his wife a widow.

FULFILMENT:

Luke 22:3. **Then entered Satan into Judas** *surnamed Iscariot, being of the number of the twelve.*
4. And he went his way, and communed with the chief priests and captains, how he might betray him unto them

Acts 1:16. Men and brethren, **this scripture must needs have been fulfilled, which the HOLY GHOST BY THE MOUTH OF DAVID SPAKE before concerning**

Judas, which was guide to them that took Jesus.
17. For he was numbered with us, and had obtained part of this ministry.
18. Now this man purchased a field with the reward of iniquity; and falling headlong, he burst asunder in the midst, and all his bowels gushed out.
*20. **For it is written in the book of Psalms, Let his habitation be desolate**, and let no man dwell therein: and **his bishoprick let another take.***

I love the way the Apostles put it...

*...which the **HOLY GHOST BY THE MOUTH OF DAVID SPAKE...***

So we see that most of what is contained in the book of Psalms was not the words of David but rather the Holy Spirit and Jesus speaking through David. Note however, that the prophetic words in Psalm and their fulfilment in the New Testament may not be exactly the same nevertheless the connection is undeniable.

Now recall the boldface words I asked you to keep in mind, *"...today have I begotten thee".*

To begot means to give birth or to father a child.

Why would God make such a statement at the baptism of Jesus? Does it mean that before that day of baptism Jesus had not been begotten of God?

That statement simply tells us that something new

35

truly happened that day to Jesus as He got baptised; the body of Jesus was reborn that day. From His birth Jesus was already known to be the Son of God but how come it was at baptism that God said *today have I begotten thee*. If Jesus was not begotten afresh that day, God would not have made that statement because God does not speak carelessly neither does He speak idle words, every word God speaks is truth. I won't be far from the truth if I say Jesus got born again of water the day He was baptised, thus showing us what we must do for our body to be born again. Did Jesus need to be born again of water? NO. Did He need to get baptised? NO. Did He need to fast? Did He need to pray? Though Jesus was God and didn't need to do all this things yet He did it as an example for us to follow, for us to see what could happen to us if we do what He did. A good leader they say leads by example, the Lord Jesus as the Good Shepherd showed that He was a Good Master by doing all these things. Jesus Christ tasted and experienced everything we have to go through for our salvation so that we can follow His example (Hebrews 4:15), He got baptised before asking us to get baptised, He prayed and fasted before teaching or asking us to do same, He preached the gospel before asking us to preach and many more, so Yes even Jesus could have been born again of water by baptism for our example.

We have seen that to begot means to make children, to give birth to or to father. We see therefore that baptism makes us children of God. God does not truly become our Father until at baptism. You are not begotten of God until you are baptised. You don't become God's own until you are baptised in water. As long as you are not baptised in water, the devil can lay claim on your body. The devil tried to take possession of the body of Moses and Joshua (Jude 1:9, Zechariah 3:1-3), he is still in the business of possessing and laying claim of people's bodies. Baptism however transfers the ownership of your body to God.

I see water baptism as a point of transfer of ownership of our body from the dominion of the devil to the dominion of God. A slave will continue to be a slave under his master unless he is set free. A sinner will remain a servant of sin until he is set free and a servant of sin is under the devil's dominion. Jesus Christ with the currency of His blood bought or redeemed the sinner from the devil, setting him free from the dominion and ownership of the devil and the exchange or claim of ownership is what happens at baptism. Have you ever wondered why at the baptism of Jesus God spoke concerning Jesus to the hearing of all that were present including the principalities and powers of darkness? It was to announce the ownership of His body as a vivid example of what happens to us at baptism. God still announces the ownership of our body at baptism to the hearing of the devil and the principalities and powers of darkness. You know first John chapter three verse eight tells us that *"He that commits sin is of the devil"*, and the devil holding unto this scripture can lay claim of your body when your body have not been washed through baptism for the remission of sins (Acts 2:38), hence the need to submit ourselves to be baptised in water, as baptism transfers the ownership of our once sinful body from the devil unto God. We must note that even though Christ has paid the price for our freedom from the bondage of sin and of the devil, if we decide not to get baptised, the devil will still lay claim of our body.

Interestingly, when God takes ownership of our body at baptism, the Godhead together give birth to a new creature. Like we have seen earlier, that whenever the Godhead come together a new thing is created. They came together at the baptism of Jesus to give birth to a new Jesus as revealed from the statement *"Today have I begotten thee",* and they still do same today for every one who gets baptised in water. We see therefore that our being born again actually takes place when we get baptised in water. That is, we actually become born again at the point of water baptism. Our new creature experience (spoken of in 2 Corinthians 5:17) begins at baptism. This I believe is what the Lord Jesus in John 3:5 referred to as born again of water.

Having established that what was prophesied by Jesus *"Thou art my Son; this day have I begotten thee"* in Psalm 2:7 is what was fulfilled when He was being baptised, we see therefore that the Lord Jesus was begotten the day He got baptised, which shows us that it is at baptism that we become God's children and God becomes our Father, it is at baptism that we are born into the kingdom of God. It is at baptism that we become Christ's.

Beloved, our new creature experience begins at baptism therefore to enjoy the new birth experience (where old things pass away and all things become new) we have to be baptised in water.

Types of Water Baptism Ordained by God

There are three types of baptism ordained by God as seen in the light of the scriptures.

They include…

1. *The Old Testament baptism.*
2. *The Forerunner baptism.*
3. *The New Testament baptism.*

1. THE OLD TESTAMENT BAPTISM (THE BAPTISM OF THE CLOUD AND SEA)

The Old Testament (OT) baptism was a reflection of things to come; it was a reflection of the New

Testament baptism (NT). The Old Testament baptism like the ordinance of blood was a shadow of the things to come; it was a shadow of the New Testament baptism. Just as the blood of bulls in the Old Testament is a reflection of the blood of Jesus Christ in the New Testament so also is the OT baptism to the NT baptism.

> *1 Corinthians 10:1. Moreover, brethren, I would not that ye should be ignorant, how that all our fathers were under the cloud, and all passed through the sea;*
> *2. And **were all baptized unto Moses in the cloud and in the sea;***

The children of Israel were in bondage in Egypt and needed to be saved from this bondage and taken to their promise land. However, note that to be totally delivered from their captors they had to go through the Red Sea which as revealed by Apostle Paul is symbolic of water baptism.

We see that although water baptism was only known or revealed to man during the time of John the Baptist yet it had been an ancient secret mystery which only God knew, such that even when man did not know or understand it, yet God still used it as a medium to disconnect His people from their past and prepare them for their promised land. I strongly feel baptism was part of the reason the children of Israel went through the Red Sea and other seas. They may not have known why they had to go through the Red Sea but by their obedience to divine instruction and leading, God led them to be baptised in the sea. Note that it was God who led the children of Israel through the Red Sea to be baptised therein.

Exodus 13:18. But God led the people about, through the way of the wilderness of the Red sea: and the children of Israel went up harnessed out of the land of Egypt.
21. And the LORD went before them by day in a pillar of a cloud, to lead them the way; and by night in a pillar of fire, to give them light; to go by day and night:

Note that they didn't go on their own volition but by divine leading. Water baptism is not a choice; it is a must for every believer who wants to be saved. The same way faith is a must to be saved by Christ is the same way water baptism is a must for salvation.

Water baptism like the Red Sea separates and delivers you from your past. Like the Pharaoh of old, your past sins will not let you go, it will keep chasing you around if you don't get baptised in water. Until you get baptised in water, your past will continue to cling to you. Water baptism washes your past off you and separates you from your past.

From scriptures we see that many things that

happened in the Old Testament are pointers to what we should experience in the New Testament.

2. THE FORERUNNER BAPTISM
(THE BAPTISM OF JOHN)

The baptism of John was the forerunner of the baptism of Jesus. John the Baptist was the forerunner of Jesus; in the same vain his baptism became the forerunner of the baptism of Jesus Christ. The baptism of John came to usher in the baptism of Jesus Christ.

Have you ever wondered why John was called the Baptist? Ordinarily he was supposed to be called John Zacharias, because he was the son of Zacharias. You will agree with me that when a man is the pioneer of a thing it is usually attributed to his name. John the Baptist was the pioneer of water Baptism and as a result of that it was attributed to his name. We see therefore that John ushered in the mystery of water Baptism as a New Testament ordinance the way he ushered in the Lord Jesus Christ.

It's interesting to note from scriptures that John the Baptist was the first to conduct water baptism as this mystery was given to Him first by God. John didn't know the Messiah, but he was to identify the Messiah through the mystery of water baptism. He came baptising men with water so that through that the Messiah would be made manifest to the people.

John 1:29. The next day John seeth Jesus coming unto him, and saith, Behold the Lamb of God, which taketh away the sin of the world.

*31. And I knew him not: but **that he should be made manifest to Israel, therefore am I come baptizing with water.***

32. And John bare record, saying, I saw the Spirit descending from heaven like a dove, and it abode upon him.

*33. And I knew him not: but **he that sent me to baptize with water, the same said unto me, Upon whom thou shalt see the Spirit descending, and remaining on him, the same is he which baptizeth with the Holy Ghost.***

It would interest you to know that, there is no record of the word baptism in the Old Testament, however before the baptism of John, the Old Testament baptism of the cloud and sea could have been God's medium for man's baptism at that time.

The baptism of John can also be called the baptism of repentance.

Mark 1:4. John did baptize in the wilderness, and preach the baptism of repentance for the remission of sins.

Luke 3:2. Annas and Caiaphas being the high priests, the word of God came unto John the

son of Zacharias in the wilderness.
3. And he came into all the country about Jordan, preaching the baptism of repentance for the remission of sins;

From scriptures we see that the baptism of John was from God, there are many justifications and witnesses to the fact that the baptism of John was from God.

Besides the scriptural references in John gospel above, we also see many other people in the Bible, including publicans testifying of the baptism of John that it was from God.

Luke 7:27. This is he, of whom it is written, Behold, I send my messenger before thy face, which shall prepare thy way before thee.
*29. And all the people that heard him, and **the publicans, justified God, being baptized with the baptism of John.***
30. But the Pharisees and lawyers rejected the counsel of God against themselves, being not baptized of him.

The Pharisees who rejected the baptism of John at that time were said to reject the counsel of God. We see therefore that rejecting water baptism is rejecting the counsel of God.

We also see from scriptures that Apollos though he

was only baptised with the baptism of John, yet was very zealous in preaching about Jesus.

Acts 18:24. And a certain Jew named Apollos, born at Alexandria, an eloquent man, and mighty in the scriptures, came to Ephesus.

25. This man was instructed in the way of the Lord; and being fervent in the spirit, he spake and taught diligently the things of the Lord, knowing only the baptism of John.

26. And he began to speak boldly in the synagogue: whom when Aquila and Priscilla had heard, they took him unto them, and expounded unto him the way of God more perfectly.

27. And when he was disposed to pass into Achaia, the brethren wrote, exhorting the disciples to receive him: who, when he was come, helped them much which had believed through grace:

28. For he mightily convinced the Jews, and that publickly, shewing by the scriptures that Jesus was Christ.

We also see that the Lord Jesus though God, allowed Himself to be baptised by John to validate John's baptism as a forerunner of the baptism of Jesus and to show us that water baptism is an essential part of our spiritual journey. Even when John the Baptist refused to baptise the Lord Jesus, He insisted that He must be baptised. If the Lord Jesus would insist to be baptised, then this goes to show us how important this mystery is to our Christian journey. I encourage you to insist on getting baptised in water just like Jesus did.

> *Matthew 3:14. But John forbad him, saying, I have need to be baptized of thee, and comest thou to me?*
> *15. And Jesus answering said unto him, **Suffer it to be so now**: for thus **it becometh us to fulfil all righteousness**. Then he suffered him.*

"...thus it becometh us to fulfil all righteousness".

In other translations the same words are translated thus...

"It is proper for us to do this to fulfil all righteousness". (New International Version)

"For we must carry out all that God requires". (New Living Translation)

"For in this way we shall do all that God requires". (Good News Translation)

"Because we must do all God wants us to do". (Contemporary English Version)

"Because this is the proper way for us to fulfil all righteousness". (International Standard Version)

In other words water baptism is necessary if we must do all that God wants us to do. I see therefore that water baptism prepares us to do the will of God, as we will see in the later chapters.

Though the baptism of John is from God we must however note that after the death of Christ at Calvary the baptism of John becomes obsolete, for *"when that which is perfect is come, then that which is in part shall be done away"*. (1 Corinthians 13:10)

The Lord Jesus is the perfect one and every mystery He brought with Him from Heaven is perfect. The baptism of Jesus is therefore a better and perfect baptism.

3. THE NEW TESTAMENT BAPTISM
   (THE BAPTISM OF JESUS CHRIST)

The New Testament baptism is the Baptism through faith in Christ. The New Testament baptism can also be referred to as the baptism of Jesus Christ. In the baptism of Jesus Christ is hidden the mystery of the remission of sin and the mystery of being born again of water. Note that the Lord Jesus came by water and blood. He came to sanctify us with water and with His blood. Not just with water or with blood but with both medium. God in His infinite wisdom gave us water and blood for our sanctification.

> *1 John 5:6. This is he that came by water and blood, even Jesus Christ; not by water only, but by water and blood. And it is the Spirit that beareth witness, because the Spirit is truth.*

Let's see this scripture from the Good News Translation (GNT).

> *1 John 5:6 (GNT). Jesus Christ is the one who came with **the water of his baptism** and the blood of his death. He came not only with the water, but with both the water and the blood. And the Spirit himself testifies that this is true, because the Spirit is truth.*

We see from the Good News Translation that the water spoken of is the water of His baptism (the New Testament Baptism).

We also see that the Holy Spirit bears witness of this truth that Jesus came by water. But where in the Bible did the Holy Spirit bear this witness?

We see this witness of the Holy Spirit when the Lord Jesus was being baptised in water.

> *Matthew 3:16. **And Jesus, when he was baptized**, went up straightway out of the*

*water: and, lo, the heavens were opened unto him, and he saw **the Spirit of God descending like a dove**, and lighting upon him:*

Before now God the Father when He sent John the Baptist to baptise men, told John that upon whom he would see the witness of the Holy Spirit, that would be the one that would baptise men with the Holy Ghost.

John 1:31. And I knew him not: but that he should be made manifest to Israel, therefore am I come baptizing with water.
*32. And John bare record, saying, **I saw the Spirit descending from heaven like a dove**, and it abode upon him.*
*33. And I knew him not: but **he that sent me to baptize with water**, the same said unto me, **Upon whom thou shalt see the Spirit descending, and remaining on him, the same is he which baptizeth with the Holy Ghost.***

Water baptism was God's medium for revealing Jesus and the Holy Spirit bore witness of this truth. We see how that the Lord Jesus came or was revealed by water and the Holy Spirit bearing witness to this truth.

Have you ever thought why water and blood came out of Jesus at Calvary when He was pierced after His death? It bears witness that Jesus came to sanctify men with water and with blood. The mystery of the water and blood from the side of Jesus bears witness to the truth that Jesus came by water and blood, to sanctify men with the water of His baptism and with His blood. The remission of sin by water and blood go hand in hand. They are from one and the same Saviour and work together for the salvation of man.

When we see the New Testament water baptism as the baptism of Jesus Christ, it becomes easy for us to understand this truth and to submit ourselves to it. Apostle Paul referred to water baptism as the circumcision of Christ such that in his letter to the Colossians (chapter two verse eleven), he reveals to us how that at baptism while we are being baptised physically here by men, the Lord Jesus is busy circumcising us spiritually. At baptism the Lord Jesus does not just look on while we get baptised but at that same moment he gets busy fixing us spiritually by removing the body of the sins of the flesh that moves us from the inside to commit sin. At baptism we do not only receive remission of past sins but that which compels us to sin is also removed from us. Jesus Christ is highly involved in the mystery of water baptism because it involved Him; it is His baptism, it is a part of Him and a part of His medium for our salvation.

After the sacrifice of Christ at Calvary only one baptism is valid, which is the baptism of Jesus Christ or the New Testament baptism. In the baptism of Jesus Christ, men are to be baptised in the name of Jesus Christ (Acts 2:38) or in the name of the Godhead (that is, In the name of the Father and of the Son and of the Holy Ghost).

Matthew 28:19. Go ye therefore, and teach all nations, **baptizing them in the name of the Father, and of the Son, and of the Holy Ghost:**

The Lord Jesus gave this commandment after His resurrection. This shows that the Sacrifice of Christ at Calvary does not nullify the mystery of water baptism; rather it empowers water baptism to be an effective medium for salvation (1 Peter 3:21).

It would interest you to know that while the Lord Jesus was here on earth His disciples conducted water baptism under His supervision. It was also believed that while the Lord Jesus lived He baptised more men than John the Baptist.

John 3:22. After these things came Jesus and his disciples into the land of Judaea; and there he tarried with them, and baptized.
23. And John also was baptizing in Aenon near to Salim, because there was much water there: and they came, and were baptized.
26. And they came unto John, and said unto him, Rabbi, he that was with thee beyond Jordan, to whom thou barest witness, behold, the same baptizeth, and all men come to him.

John 4:1. When therefore the Lord knew how the Pharisees had heard that Jesus made and baptized more disciples than John,

2. (Though Jesus himself baptized not, but his disciples,)

3. He left Judaea, and departed again into Galilee.

The Lord Jesus did not only supervise the baptism of men while here on earth, we also see Him after His resurrection in Acts 22:10-16 recommending the New Testament water baptism (His baptism) to Saul and also to everyone who believes, when He announced the great commission (Matthew 28:19, Mark 16:15-16).

The New Testament baptism is a must for every New Testament believer. Therefore every New Testament believer must be baptised with the baptism of Jesus Christ, in the name of the Father and of the Son and of the Holy Ghost. Apostle Paul's encounter with the Ephesian brethren reflects this truth. The Ephesian brethren were baptised with the baptism of John and as a result of that they could not receive the Holy Ghost. They had to get baptised again with the baptism of Jesus before they could receive the Holy Ghost. Jesus Christ baptises with the Holy Ghost and being baptised in water in His name prepares us for this baptism of the Holy Ghost.

Acts 19:2. He said unto them, **Have ye received the Holy Ghost since ye believed?** *And they said unto him, We have not so much as heard whether there be any Holy Ghost.*
3. And he said unto them, **Unto what then were ye baptized? And they said, Unto John's baptism.**
4. Then said Paul, John verily baptized with the baptism of repentance, saying unto the people, that they should believe on him which should come after him, that is, on Christ Jesus.
5. **When they heard this, they were baptized in the name of the Lord Jesus.**
6. **And when Paul had laid his hands upon them, the Holy Ghost came on them;** *and they spake with tongues, and prophesied.*

The baptism of John limited the Ephesian brethren from receiving the Holy Ghost but thank God for their willingness to be rebaptised with the baptism of Christ, and thank God apostle Paul knew the reason why they could not receive the Holy Ghost before his arrival. The Ephesian brethren did not hesitate to get baptised again when they heard the truth, my prayer is that you will not hesitate to get baptised aright as you read this truth about water baptism.

Many believers get worried about getting baptised a second time, but what we should worry more about should be about getting it right. I believe God will not punish anyone for getting baptised more that once just to ensure that they get it right.

We see from the above scripture that water baptism is necessary for the baptism of the Holy Ghost. I strongly believe that the disciples of Jesus Christ were able to receive the Holy Ghost in the upper room because they were first baptised in water.

Dear reader, the New Testament baptism or the baptism of Jesus Christ is a must for every New Testament believer. Don't hesitate to get it right with the mystery of water baptism.

From this point forth in this book, wherever water baptism is mentioned, please be reminded that it refers to the New Testament baptism of Jesus Christ.

Mode of Water Baptism

HOW SHOULD WATER BAPTISM BE DONE?

The word BAPTISM itself tells us how it should be done. Baptism is a transliteration of the Greek word *Baptízō* which means to dip or immerse. In otherwords to be truly baptised, we must be immersed in water completely from head to toe.

Water baptism is not a church denominational doctrine, it is a direct command from Jesus that every Christian must observe to do and as such no church (nor its leaders) have the exclusive right to baptise, neither is there any church leader that should say water baptism is not necessary. It is important to note that, it is not about the church where you get baptised, it is about doing it right according to the dictates and instructions of scriptures. The Ethiopian eunuch whom Philip baptised by the leading of the Holy Ghost was not baptised in a church, he was returning from his church when Philip met him on the road, preached to him and baptised him. He was baptised on the way while travelling without even entering any church. No church was involved, just a man with the gospel and full of the Holy Ghost. I therefore believe that any Spirit filled preacher of the gospel, who himself has been baptised can baptise.

Water baptism as spiritual burial

Understanding water baptism as a spiritual burial paints a true picture of how water baptism should be done. We see from scriptures that water baptism is a form of spiritual burial.

> *Romans 6:4. Therefore we are **buried with him by baptism** into death: that like as Christ was raised up from the dead by the glory of the Father, even so we also should **walk in newness of life**.*
> *Colossians 2:12. **Buried with him in baptism**, wherein also ye are risen with him through the faith of the operation of God, who hath raised him from the dead.*

Buried with him by baptism…
Buried with him in baptism…

We therefore see that water baptism is God's medium for burying us with Christ (or for identifying with the burial and resurrection of Christ).

Understanding water baptism as burial gives us so much insight into how baptism should be done. In burial the right way to bury is to put the object to be buried completely inside the grave or burial medium. In the case of water baptism, water is the burial medium. You will agree with me that when someone is being buried in a grave, they are buried (or put in the grave) completely from crown to toe, in other words it would be abnormal and wrong to bury someone head only, torso only or legs only with the other parts dangling outside the grave. Now, just as it is abnormal and wrong to bury a man half way (whether head only, torso only or leg only), the same applies to water baptism when we are not completely immersed in the water or burial medium.

You know many people use the excuse of whatever we do in faith is what matters to justify being baptised by affusion or aspersion but we must understand that no amount of faith we express can change God's word because faith itself is a product of God's word and depends on God's word to deliver results, *for faith comes by hearing God's word* (*Romans 10:17*). We must always remember that faith depends on the word of God, and that anything done outside God's prescribed word is not faith.

Another excuse ministers give for baptism by

aspersion and affusion is that this form of baptism is meant for the sick, but how come those who get baptised via this medium today are the very healthy ones in the church? Some say it's due to the availability of water, but that is not an excuse because the God who put rivers in every corner of the earth even in the desert for our easy access has a purpose for it. Jesus Christ and John the Baptist had to go to a city where there was much water to baptise people (John 3:22,23). No excuse is enough to modify God's instruction. You know just a little alteration to the truth makes it half-truth, and half-truth is as deadly as a lie. The devil knows exactly how to sell this deadly half-truth to men; he even tried it with the Lord Jesus.

Let's stop accepting excuses and follow the example of Jesus Christ. Let's follow the truth written in the Holy Scriptures. Jesus was baptised by immersion, let's follow His perfect example.

Dearly beloved, it's better to be right than not, do it right today.

Get baptised by immersion in the name of the Father, Son and of the Holy Ghost.

Remember, to live holy while here on earth we need to be baptised in water.

Do you truly want to enter heaven?

Then get baptised in water.

Secure God's approval.

Get your body circumcised.

Receive power to live holy.

Water Baptism as a Spiritual Circumcision

*Colossians 2:11. In whom also ye are circumcised with the **circumcision made without hands**, in putting off the body of the sins of the flesh by **the circumcision of Christ**:*
12. Buried with him in baptism, wherein also ye are risen with him through the faith of the operation of God, who hath raised him from the dead.

Circumcision is the removal of the foreskin of the flesh, that is, the removal of the hard and insensitive part of the skin. Water baptism is a spiritual circumcision: a circumcision made without human hands, a circumcision made by Jesus Christ himself. At baptism the Lord Jesus circumcises us with a circumcision called the circumcision of Christ. So while we are being baptised physically here by men, Jesus is also busy circumcising us spiritually at the same time, removing the body of the sins of the flesh from off our body. This body of the sins of the flesh also called the nature of sin is what moves and compels us to sin even when we don't want to, but thank God it is removed at baptism from our body. If we were to see this circumcision I feel it would be like skinning the entire body. I would therefore say at baptism we are spiritually skinned to remove the part of our body that is susceptible to sin. Without the circumcision of baptism we are susceptible and easily attracted to sin. I believe part of the reason God commanded man (through Abraham) to be circumcised physically was for us to understand the spiritual circumcision that happens at baptism. Water Baptism is the spiritual replica of the physical circumcision of the flesh commanded through Abraham.

> *Genesis 17:11. And ye shall circumcise the flesh of your foreskin; and it shall be a token of the covenant betwixt me and you.*

In this light, we see that baptism as a circumcision brings us into a covenant with God. At baptism we come into a spiritual union and covenant with God. We commit God to be the LORD and Saviour of our life. We commit God to secure our salvation and spiritual destiny as seen in Mark 16:16, where it is written that those who are baptised *"shall be saved"*.

Also baptism as a circumcision regenerates us and delivers us from stiffneckedness and spiritual obstinacy.

Deuteronomy 10:16. Circumcise therefore the foreskin of your heart, and be no more stiffnecked.

When the insensitive part of us is removed at baptism, we become pliable and flexible to divine guidance.

Water baptism as a circumcision also enables us to love God with all our heart and soul. Note that, when God commands us to do a thing He always makes available the necessary enablement or ability to do as He commands. God commands us to love Him with all our heart and soul (Mark 12:30) and water baptism is God's medium for the spiritual enablement to love God as He commands.

*Deuteronomy 30:6. And **the LORD thy God will circumcise thine heart**, and the heart of thy seed, to love the LORD thy God with all thine heart, and with all thy soul, that thou mayest live.*

The LORD thy God will circumcise thine heart…

This I believe reveals why the Lord Jesus has to circumcise us with a circumcision made without hands at baptism. This circumcision empowers us to love God with all our heart and soul. Until our heart is circumcised we cannot love God as He commands. If water baptism is a spiritual circumcision as documented in the Holy Bible then we need it if we must love God with all our heart, mind, soul, body and strength.

Water baptism as a spiritual circumcision prepares us for the Promised Land (Heaven). Circumcision prepared the children of Israel for the Promised Land.

> *Joshua 5:2. At that time the LORD said unto Joshua, Make thee sharp knives, and* **circumcise again the children of Israel the second time.**
>
> *3. And Joshua made him sharp knives, and circumcised the children of Israel at the hill of the foreskins.*
>
> *4. And this is the cause why Joshua did circumcise: All the people that came out of Egypt, that were males, even all the men of war, died in the wilderness by the way, after they came out of Egypt.*
>
> *5. Now all the people that came out were circumcised: but all the people that were born in the wilderness by the way as they came*

forth out of Egypt, them they had not circumcised.

7. And their children, whom he raised up in their stead, them Joshua circumcised: for they were uncircumcised, because they had not circumcised them by the way.

8. And it came to pass, when they had done circumcising all the people, that they abode in their places in the camp, till they were whole.

*9. And **the LORD said unto Joshua, This day have I rolled away the reproach of Egypt from off you.** Wherefore the name of the place is called Gilgal unto this day.*

13. And it came to pass, when Joshua was by Jericho, that he lifted up his eyes and looked, and, behold, there stood a man over against him with his sword drawn in his hand: and Joshua went unto him, and said unto him, Art thou for us, or for our adversaries?

*14. And he said, Nay; but **as captain of the host of the LORD am I now come.** And Joshua fell on his face to the earth, and did worship, and said unto him, What saith my lord unto his servant?*

15. And the captain of the LORD's host said unto Joshua, Loose thy shoe from off thy foot; for the place whereon thou standest is holy. And Joshua did so.

The same way circumcision prepared the children of Israel for the Promised Land, God sent John the Baptist with the mystery of water baptism to prepare us for Jesus and Heaven.

Note from the above scriptures that the place where the children of Israel were circumcised was called Gilgal. Gilgal was where the Israelites first encamped after crossing Jordan to enter the Promised Land (Joshua 4:19). At Gilgal they were circumcised again the second time, in other words they renewed their earlier covenant of circumcision with God. At Gilgal God rolled away the reproach of Egypt from off the children of Israel, that is, at Gilgal the disgrace and shame the children of Israel suffered at Egypt was removed. Also at Gilgal after the circumcision of the children of Israel, God sent an angel as a captain to fight for the children of Israel. In this light Gilgal can be seen as a place of new beginnings, a place of renewed covenant and commitment, a transition point for the children of Israel, a point where God took over their battle. All these pictures of Gilgal reflect what happens when we are spiritually circumcised at baptism.

We must also note that spiritual uncircumcision is part of the reason God's wrath is coming upon man. To escape God's wrath and fury we must be spiritually circumcised through baptism.

Jeremiah 4:4. **Circumcise yourselves to the LORD***, and take away the foreskins of your heart, ye men of Judah and inhabitants of Jerusalem:* **lest my fury come forth like fire, and burn that none can quench it***, because of the evil of your doings.*

From the above scripture we understand that we can circumcise ourselves unto God, in other words we separate ourselves unto God through the spiritual circumcision at baptism. By submitting ourselves to the circumcision of water baptism we separate ourselves unto God. We see therefore that water baptism separates us unto God; it prepares us to become vessels for God's use. As exemplified in the life and ministry of the Lord Jesus, as soon as He was baptised, He became anointed, separated, empowered and commissioned for the kick off of His ministry on the earth (Luke 4:1-21).

Benefits of Water Baptism

The benefits of water baptism to a believer are numerous. Among many things, here are some benefits of water baptism and what it does to a believer.

#1: WATER BAPTISM BRINGS US INTO CHRIST
AND UNITES US WITH HIM.

Baptism brings us into a spiritual union with Christ, it is symbolic of a Christian's spiritual union with Christ in His death, burial and resurrection (Romans 6:3-7). In other words we come into Christ at baptism. We see therefore that we are not in Christ until we are baptised because baptism is what brings us into Christ. Baptism is what brings us out of darkness into the marvellous light of Christ. It is what brings us out of the kingdom of the devil into the kingdom of God.

We must understand that we are baptised into Christ, that is, we come into Christ BY baptism. We don't just speak or confess our way into Christ, rather we get baptised into Christ.

The scriptures below will help our understanding.

> *Romans 6:3. Know ye not, that so many of us as were **baptized into Jesus Christ** were **baptized into his death?***

> *Galatians 3:27. For as many of you as have been **baptized into Christ** have put on Christ.*

Note the words ***baptised into…***

We see from the above scriptures that to be a part of the body of Christ, we have to be baptised into it. To come into Christ we have to be baptised into Him, to be a part of Christ we must be baptised in water.

When the Lord Jesus washed the feet of His disciples, He revealed to us how that washing our body with water is necessary for us to become a part of Him, to come into Him or to belong to Him. He said to Peter, unless I wash you, you would not belong to me or become a part of me. He went further to tell the disciples to follow His example.

Let's take a look at the scriptures below.

John 13:3. Jesus knowing that the Father had given all things into his hands, and that he was come from God, and went to God;

4. He riseth from supper, and laid aside his garments; and took a towel, and girded himself.

5. After that he poureth water into a bason, and began to wash the disciples' feet, and to wipe them with the towel wherewith he was girded.

6. Then cometh he to Simon Peter: and Peter saith unto him, Lord, dost thou wash my feet?

7. Jesus answered and said unto him, ***What I do thou knowest not now; but thou shalt know hereafter.***

8. Peter saith unto him, Thou shalt never wash my feet. Jesus answered him, ***If I wash thee not, thou hast no part with me.***

10. Jesus saith to him, He that is washed needeth not save to wash his feet, but is clean every whit: and ye are clean, but not all.

13. Ye call me Master and Lord: and ye say well; for so I am.

14. If I then, your Lord and Master, have washed your feet; ye also ought to ***wash one another's feet.***

15. For I have given you an example, that ye should do as I have done to you.

16. Verily, verily, I say unto you, ***The servant is not greater than his lord; neither he that is sent greater than he that sent him.***

17. *If ye know these things, happy are ye if ye do them.*

Here's how the New Living Translation puts verse 8 of the above scripture.

John 13:8. (NLT). "No," Peter protested, "you will never ever wash my feet!" Jesus replied, "Unless I wash you, you won't belong to me."

The Lord Jesus was saying to Peter, if I don't wash you, you won't belong to me, neither would you enjoy what I have in store for you. The Lord Jesus was showing us how important it is to be washed with physical water. Through that scripture the Lord Jesus is saying to everyone in this present day, who is rejecting His counsel to be baptised, who is saying "No" I don't need water baptism to be saved, that if He doesn't wash you through water baptism, you won't belong to Him, neither can you enjoy what He has done for you at Calvary. It's important to note that though man may be baptising you here in the physical, the Lord Jesus is perfecting it in the spiritual. Colossians 2:11-12 reveals to us that when we are baptised we are being circumcised with the circumcision of Christ, which is a circumcision made without hands, in other words when we are being baptised here physically, the Lord Jesus is there in the spirit realm circumcising us.

It's important to note that the Lord Jesus was not

teaching the disciples humility by washing their feet, rather He was unveiling to them a mystery that they must all engage and pass on to the next generation. Jesus as the Master washed the feet of the servants, to let us know that no church leader should think they are too anointed to baptise others or too anointed to be baptised themselves. We can't be too anointed than Jesus, as anointed as the Lord Jesus was yet He still submitted Himself to be baptised, this I believe is to show us the importance of water baptism.

Note the following from the scriptures in John 13.

- *The disciples through the washing of water became a part of Jesus, that is, they belonged to Jesus after being washed with water.*
- *The disciples needed to be washed with water to be made clean.*
- *Jesus washed the feet of the disciple so they also could wash the feet of others.*
- *Jesus washed the disciples feet as an example for us to do as he has done to us*
- *No servant is greater than his Master; neither he that is sent greater than he that sent him.*

The servant is not greater than his Lord...

The Lord Jesus is saying we can't know or understand scriptures more than Him who is the Living Word. He did the dying on the cross and the same He, is saying we must be baptised. If we refuse to get baptised we are saying that we know better than Him.

The sent cannot be greater or know better than he that sent him. The Lord Jesus commissioned us and sent us into every nation to preach the gospel and baptise those who believe in the gospel. If we along the line refuse to baptise those that believe after we have preached the gospel to them, because we think we understand grace and think that with grace we don't need baptism, we show ourselves to know better than Jesus who gave us grace and still instructed us to baptise and be baptised. If Jesus who gave us grace says we should be baptised in other to be saved (Mark 16:16), who is man to say baptism is not necessary. If the sender or master says you need baptism to be saved who is the sent or messenger to say, you don't need baptism to be saved. Beloved, you can't be greater than your master or he that sent you. The devil tried it and he lost even that which he had and is still living in that regret to date and till forever. Don't let that be your portion by not doing what God commanded you to do. You can loss your heavenly place like the devil by not being baptised and by discouraging others from being baptised.

If Jesus our master was baptised, who are we to say we would not be baptised. We can't know more than Jesus or be more anointed than Him. If we refuse to get baptised as he exemplified to us, then we make ourselves greater than Jesus, which is a reflection of pride and the proud have no place in God's kingdom. Moreso, do not forget that grace is not given to the proud (James 4:6). A man who rejects God's counsel or instruction cannot receive grace from God.

From the feet washing mystery we see that the disciples only needed their feet to be washed in other to be made completely clean. Now note that when being baptised by immersion, the feet of those to be baptised (or made clean) is in the water, which is not so with those who are baptised by sprinkling, aspersion or affusion. Our feet just being in the water fulfils what the Lord Jesus did to the disciples to make them clean every whit, this however can not be achieved in baptism by aspersion and affusion, which further invalidates these mode of baptism.

You know, people love to claim the blessings of God without doing what they need to do to enjoy the blessings. And you know the Holy Bible says in 2 Corinthians 5:17 that *if any man be **in** Christ, he is a new creature: old things are passed away; behold, all things are become new,* (and many believers love to proclaim this), however I would like to say that this scripture is only fulfilled when we get baptised in water. In otherwords, we can only have the new creature experience when we get baptised in water, because it is at baptism that we come into Christ.

Please note very importantly that, if you are not baptised in water, you are not yet in Christ, which simply means that you are still in darkness and under the dominion of the devil. No matter how much you believe in Jesus Christ and even confess Him as your Lord and Saviour, if you are not baptised in water, you are not yet in Christ. Remember, your faith in Christ is dead without the action of water baptism.

Beloved, the need for water baptism cannot be overemphasised. Please make haste and get baptised into Christ.

#2: WATER BAPTISM BEARS WITNESS OF OUR REPENTANCE, FAITH AND SALVATION IN CHRIST HERE ON THE EARTH.

Water baptism bears witness of your repentance, faith and salvation in Christ here on the earth.

> *1 John 5:6. This is he that* **came by water and blood, even Jesus Christ**; *not by water only, but by water and blood.* **And it is the Spirit that beareth witness**, *because the Spirit is truth.*
> *7. For there are three that bear record in heaven, the Father, the Word, and the Holy Ghost: and these three are one.*
> *8. And there are three that bear witness in earth, the* **spirit**, *and the* **water**, *and the* **blood**: *and these three agree in one.*
> *9. If we receive the witness of men, the witness of God is greater: for this is the witness of God*

which he hath testified of his Son.
10. He that believeth on the Son of God hath the
witness in himself: he that believeth not God hath
made him a liar; because he believeth not the
record that God gave of his Son.

There are three witnesses in heaven and three on the earth that must bear witness of our faith and salvation in Jesus Christ. In heaven, God the Father, God the Son and God the Holy Ghost bear witness of our salvation in Christ. Here on the earth three things also bear witness of our salvation in Christ. They include our spirit, water baptism and the blood of Jesus Christ.

Let's take a look at them one after the other.

THE WITNESS OF OUR OWN SPIRIT...

Our spirit stands as a witness to attest to our faith and salvation in Christ. If our spirit does not have that inner witness that we are the children of God, then we are not.

We see in 1 John 5:10 that *he that believeth on the Son of God hath the witness in himself,* in other words our spirit will always bear witness of our faith in Christ.

With the Lord Jesus as our perfect example, we see Him in John 8:18 showing us how that His own spirit bears witness of Himself and how that the Father also bears witness of Him, thus pointing us to an earthly witness and a heavenly witness concerning Him.

John 8:18. I am one that bear witness of myself, and the Father that sent me beareth witness of me.

THE WITNESS OF WATER BAPTISM...

As seen in verse 1 John 5:10, when you believe in Jesus as the Son of God, your spirit bears witness of this, in other words only you can attest to your faith in Christ, nevertheless personal witness is not enough, other people need to also bear witness of your salvation, and this happens when you get baptised in water. In Hebrews 12:1 Apostle Paul reminds us that we are compassed about with a great cloud of human witnesses, principalities and powers of darkness inclusive.

The Lord Jesus shows us in John 10:25 that the works we do can bear witness of our faith, and baptism is one of those works that bears witness of our faith in Christ here on the earth.

John 10:25. Jesus answered them, I told you, and ye believed not: the works that I do in my Father's name, they bear witness of me.

At baptism we identify with the death and resurrection of Christ (Romans 6:3-5), therefore if we say we believe in Christ and yet do not identify with His death and resurrection through water baptism, it makes our faith of no value. Water baptism bears witness that we have validated our faith in Christ and have identified with the sacrifice of Christ at Calvary.

Water baptism bears witness that our body has been washed with the washing of regeneration for our spiritual rebirth. It bears witness that we belong to Christ spirit, soul and body.

We also see that the Lord Jesus came with two witnesses: the witness of His water baptism and the witness of the blood of His death, to bear witness of our salvation in Him.

1 John 5:6 (GNT). Jesus Christ is the one who came with the water of his baptism and the blood of his death. He came not only with the water, but with both the water and the blood. And the Spirit himself testifies that this is true, because the Spirit is truth.

In other words, water baptism and the blood of Jesus are Christ's medium for our salvation from sin. They bear witness here on earth of our being saved by Christ.

Now, let's see how that the blood bears witness of our salvation in Christ.

THE WITNESS OF THE BLOOD...

John 6:53. Then Jesus said unto them, Verily, verily, I say unto you, Except ye eat the flesh of the Son of man, and drink his blood, ye have no life in you.
54. Whoso eateth my flesh, and drinketh my blood, hath eternal life; and I will raise him up at the last day.

The blood bears witness that our spirit has been purged with the blood of Jesus Christ, that the price for our salvation has been paid and we have been redeemed.

We see from the above scripture that the witness of the blood is what will guarantee our resurrection on the last day, and for this blood to witness for you it must be in you, you must drink it. The blood of Jesus Christ imparts in us the eternal life of Christ and this is what will bear witness for our resurrection on the last day. Without the blood of Jesus Christ in you, you cannot have eternal life, and without the blood in you to bear witness of the eternal life of Christ in you, you can't be raised on the last day. On the last day Jesus will be looking out for those who have His blood in them to raise them up.

The Lord Jesus came to give us eternal life as recorded in John 3:16, but know that without drinking His blood you can't have this eternal life. You receive the eternal life that Jesus Christ promised in John 3:16 when you drink His blood, *for Whoso drinketh my blood HATH eternal life...* Please note the word HATH.

It's erroneous to believe John 3:16 and expect eternal life, if we do not do what John 6:54 says. John 3:16 promises us eternal life if we believe in Christ but we actually receive the eternal life when we eat the flesh and drink the blood of Jesus Christ as seen in John 6:54.

You can't receive eternal life by just believing John 3:16, you must do what is written in John 6:54 to receive eternal life. In other words, we can't receive eternal life by just mentally believing in Jesus Christ as our Saviour, we must eat His flesh and drink His blood. The eternal life Jesus gives is in His blood *(for the life of the flesh is in the blood)* and this blood will attest or bear witness to our faith in Christ and empower us to be raised on the last day.

To believe in Jesus Christ as our Saviour and not express the same in our works makes our faith invalid and dead (James 2:17,18,20,26), because faith is actually expressed through our works or actions.

Remember the life of the flesh is in the blood (Leviticus 17:11), in other words the eternal life of Jesus Christ is in His blood therefore to have this eternal life in us we must drink His blood.

Faith begins with a mental and spiritual acceptance of the truth and can further be expressed physically as works, in other words works (which I refer to as the works of faith) is the physical expression of faith.

We have seen how that God has given us physical mediums to bear witness of our salvation in Christ and water baptism is one of such medium. Whether we like it or not, believe it or not, accept it or not, the truth remains that water baptism will be there on the last day to bear witness of our salvation in Christ on the earth, it will be there to attest to whether we identified with the death and resurrection of Christ through baptism while we were on the earth. My prayer is that its witness will not be against you.

#3: WATER BAPTISM GRANTS US REMISSION OF SINS.

> *Acts 2:38. Then Peter said unto them, Repent, and* **be baptized every one of you in the name of Jesus Christ for the remission of sins**, *and ye shall receive the gift of the Holy Ghost.*

Remission means pardon or forgiveness of sins.
Interestingly, after we repent we must get baptised in water to receive forgiveness of our sins. When we see water baptism as an expression or demonstration of faith, it becomes easy to understand why we must get baptised to receive the forgiveness of our sins through our faith in the death and resurrection of Christ.

#4: WATER BAPTISM WASHES AWAY OUR SINS.

*Acts 22:16. And now why tarriest thou? arise, and **be baptized, and wash away thy sins**, calling on the name of the Lord.*

Water baptism is one of God's tools for washing the sins of man. This point is similar to point three above. Note from the above scripture the urgency of the need to get baptised, *"Why tarriest thou?"*, therefore, we must not waste time in getting baptised.

#5: WATER BAPTISM OPEN US UP TO RECEIVE THE HOLY GHOST & GRACE.

Baptism opens you up to other graces, or gifts of the Spirit that you need to live a sanctified life.

*Acts 2:38. Then Peter said unto them, Repent, and **be baptized** every one of you in the name of Jesus Christ for the remission of sins, **and ye shall receive the gift of the Holy Ghost.***

...be baptised and ye shall receive the gift of the Holy Ghost.

In other words if you are not baptised, you will not receive the gift of the Holy Ghost. The Ephesian brethren in Acts 19 could not receive the Holy Ghost until they were baptised in the name of Christ.

#6: AT BAPTISM GOD PUTS A SEAL OF APPROVAL ON OUR SONSHIP

Baptism among other things puts a seal on your acceptance of Jesus Christ. Jesus Christ as an example for us to follow had to be baptised in water to show us what we must do and as He was being baptised God gave His node of approval by saying Jesus was His beloved Son.

> *Matthew 3:13. Then cometh Jesus from Galilee to Jordan unto John, to be baptized of him.*
> *14. But John forbad him, saying, I have need to be baptized of thee, and comest thou to me?*
> *15. And Jesus answering said unto him, Suffer it to be so now: for thus it becometh us to fulfil all righteousness. Then he suffered him.*
> *16. And Jesus, when he was baptized, went up straightway out of the water: and, lo, the heavens were opened unto him, and he saw the Spirit of God descending like a dove, and lighting upon him:*
> *17. And lo a voice from heaven, saying, **This is my beloved Son**, in whom I am well pleased.*

From this event I see that God the Father speaks into our destiny at baptism. He puts His seal of approval upon us as we get baptised. God's seal of approval came upon Jesus Christ after He was baptised in water, in the same manner at water baptism God puts His seal of approval upon our life as His own children. We may not hear this kind of audible approval when someone gets baptised in water but I strongly believe that there is an expression of approval in heaven and in the realm of the spirit when any soul gets baptised in water, *for there is joy in heaven over one sinner that repents* (Luke 15:10), we may not see it but it happens.

For your faith in Christ to be approved of God you must be baptised in water. When we believe in Jesus Christ and our faith is validated by baptism, we receive a seal of approval that we belong to God.

Do not forget that when you were in the world wallowing in sin, you were a child of the devil (1 John 3:8) but God needs to reverse that when you accept Jesus Christ as your Lord and Saviour by openly approving you as His son or daughter. And the ordinance of baptism is God's mystery for openly declaring you as His to the devil, the principalities and powers of darkness and the entire world. At baptism we do not only openly identify with Jesus but God also openly identifies with us.

#7: BAPTISM CIRCUMCISES OUR FLESH TO ENABLE US OVERCOME SIN.

Colossians 2:11. ***In whom also ye are circumcised with the circumcision made without hands****, in putting off the body of the sins of the flesh by the circumcision of Christ:*

12. ***Buried with him in baptism****, wherein also ye are risen with him through the faith of the operation of God, who hath raised him from the dead.*

13. And you, being dead in your sins and the uncircumcision of your flesh, hath he quickened together with him, having forgiven you all trespasses;

Circumcision is the removal of the hard insensitive part of the skin to expose the soft, tender, sensitive part, in other words the circumcision of baptism makes you sensitive to the leading of the Holy Spirit and also makes your flesh subjective to your spirit. Without the circumcision of baptism you cannot put your body under the subjection or leading of the Holy Spirit. Without the spiritual circumcision of water baptism you won't be sensitive to the leading of the Holy Ghost, neither can your flesh overcome sin because your uncircumcised flesh cannot be put under the subjection of the spirit.

At baptism, the body of the sins of the flesh (that is the lustful part of man which makes man sensitive to the sins or lusts of the flesh) is removed. Note that the body of the sins of the flesh (which I also see as the lustful part of man) is what causes man to lust after the flesh and commit the sins of the flesh seen in Galatians 5:16-21 and this part of man always resists the actions and leading of the Holy Spirit. That is why it is very important for this part of man to be removed through the spiritual circumcision that happens at baptism if we must overcome the lust of the flesh, walk in the Spirit and live holy while here on earth.

It's important to note that in the circumcision of baptism, every part of your body must be circumcised; otherwise you will not be able to put every part of your body under subjection.

Please note that, by this insight if you are baptised by sprinkling (aspersions) or just by pouring water on your head (affusion), then I suppose only your head has been circumcised and only your head can be put under subjection.

#8: WATER BAPTISM CRUCIFIES THE BODY OF SIN IN US AND MAKES US DEAD TO SIN.

Water baptism makes us dead to sin: it destroys the tendencies and passion to sin in us, so that we can live a holy life (Romans 6:4,6).

Water Baptism is God's mystery for making our

bodies to be insensitive and uncooperative to sinful desires. It helps us to mortify or control our bodies (Colossians 3:1-5) in other to live righteous.

Romans 6:3. Know ye not, that so many of us as were baptized into Jesus Christ were baptized into his death?

*4. Therefore we are **buried with him by baptism into death**: that like as Christ was raised up from the dead by the glory of the Father, even so we also should walk in newness of life.*

5. For if we have been planted together in the likeness of his death, we shall be also in the likeness of his resurrection:

*6. Knowing this, that **our old man is crucified with him, that the body of sin might be destroyed, that henceforth we should not serve sin.***

7. For he that is dead is freed from sin.

Our old man is crucified with Christ, that the body of sin might be destroyed, that henceforth we should not serve sin.

The body of sin is destroyed at baptism so that sin should no more have power over us. We see from scriptures that the uncircumcised sinful part of our body is destroyed when we get baptised in water, so that we can live a holy life while here on earth.

Baptism crucifies and destroys the body of sin in us, so that we don't have to serve sin anymore. Through baptism we are able to put under subjection our flesh alongside its affections and lusts, thereby overcoming the lusts of our flesh.

Every time we commit a sin of the flesh, we are serving sin. But what are these sins of the flesh we are talking about? Apostle Paul by the Holy Spirit reveals them to us.

*Galatians 5:19. Now the works of the flesh are manifest, which are these; **Adultery, fornication, uncleanness, lasciviousness,***
20. Idolatry, witchcraft, hatred, variance, emulations, wrath, strife, seditions, heresies,
***21. Envyings, murders, drunkenness, revellings**, and such like: of the which I tell you before, as I have also told you in time past, that they which do such things shall not inherit the kingdom of God.*
*24. And **they that are Christ's have crucified the flesh with the affections and lusts.***

By the crucifixion of our flesh through water baptism, we are empowered and made able to overcome all the above works of the flesh.

#9: WATER BAPTISM EMPOWERS YOU TO PUT ON THE NATURE OF CHRIST.

When you get baptised and your sinful old body is destroyed, you become empowered to put on Christ.

Galatians 3:27. For as many of you as have been baptized into Christ have put on Christ.

When we put on Christ people see the glory of God upon us, this was what made the early apostles to be called Christians because they became Christlike in nature. By putting on Christ we are expected to manifest the nature of Christ, His meekness, love, compassion, fervency etc.

#10: WATER BAPTISM GRANTS US ACCESS TO GOD AND TO HEAVEN.

*John 3:5. Jesus answered, Verily, verily, I say unto thee, **Except a man be born of water** and of the Spirit, **he cannot enter into the kingdom of God.***

The Lord Jesus made it clear that without being born of water, no man can enter the kingdom of God. This point has already been dealt with in detail in chapter one.

However looking at the baptism of the Lord Jesus, we also see a connection between water baptism and heaven, how that we experience an open heaven at water baptism.

> *Matthew 3:16.* ***And Jesus, when he was baptized,*** *went up straightway out of the water: and, lo,* ***the heavens were opened unto him****, and he saw the Spirit of God descending like a dove, and lighting upon him:*
> *17. And lo a voice from heaven, saying, This is my beloved Son, in whom I am well pleased.*

The heavens were opened unto Jesus as He got baptised. I believe the heavens are opened unto us as well when we get baptised.

One important thing water baptism does for us is that, it circumcises us and makes us sensitive to the leading of the Holy Ghost, which consequently enables us to live a holy life while here on earth in preparation for heaven. Without the circumcision of baptism we will not be sensitive to the leading of the Holy Ghost, neither can we live a holy life.

> *Romans 8:8. So then* ***they that are in the flesh cannot please God.***
> *13. For if ye live after the flesh, ye shall die: but* ***if ye through the Spirit do mortify the deeds of the body, ye shall live.***
> *14. For as many as are led by the Spirit of God, they are the sons of God.*

*Galatians 5:16. This I say then, **Walk in the Spirit, and ye shall not fulful the lust of the flesh.***

19. Now the works of the flesh are manifest, which are these; Adultery, fornication, uncleanness, lasciviousness,

20. Idolatry, witchcraft, hatred, variance, emulations, wrath, strife, seditions, heresies,

*21. Envyings, murders, drunkenness, revellings, and such like: of the which I tell you before, as I have also told you in time past, that **they which do such things shall not inherit the kingdom of God.***

Through the leading of the Holy Ghost we overcome all the sins that would hinder us from entering heaven. Water baptism gives us the ability to say "NO" to sin and to allow our flesh to be led by the Holy Spirit in other to live a holy life on earth in preparation for heaven.

It's important to say at this point that, water baptism does not get us immune to temptations. When we believe in Jesus and are baptised in water, our body does not automatically get immune to temptations but we receive the ability to say "NO" to temptations. One difference between those who are baptised and those who are not is that, those who are not baptised in water do not have the ability to resist or say "NO" to temptations. Faith in Christ and water baptism does not stop the devil from tempting us, but it empowers us to resist the devil and say "NO" to his temptations to sin. The Lord Jesus was tempted as soon as He was baptised, you too will be tempted even after you get baptised, but the good news is that you have the power to resist the temptations. I have to say this because many believers feel after they get born again they should be totally immune to temptations and when they feel their body still being enticed and tempted to sin after a while they get discouraged. The truth remains that as long as we live in this body we would be tempted to sin and we would be in a constant battle with our flesh, but the good news remains that we have the power to overcome every temptation to sin and to put our body under subjection as we prepare for heaven while here on the earth.

Chapter

7

Grace, Faith and Baptism

You know many Christians say water baptism is not necessary for salvation and to support their claim they quote *we are saved by grace through faith*, forgetting that the Lord Jesus had said *he that believeth and is baptised shall be saved.*

I do not understand, how that the one who died on the cross and paid the price says you need faith and baptism to be saved immediately after His resurrection from the dead, whereas those who do not even know what it takes to die on the cross are saying all you need is faith, and they quote we are saved by grace through faith. Clearly many who preach this saved by grace through faith gospel do not even understand what grace and faith is.

Perhaps they would have missed the following scriptures about faith.

Mark 16:15. And he said unto them, Go ye into all the world, and preach the gospel to every creature.
16. He that believeth and is baptized shall be saved; but he that believeth not shall be damned.

James 2:14. What doth it profit, my brethren, though a man say he hath faith, and have not works? can faith save him?
17. Even so faith, if it hath not works, is dead, being alone.
18. Yea, a man may say, Thou hast faith, and I have works: shew me thy faith without thy works, and I will shew thee my faith by my works.
19. Thou believest that there is one God; thou doest well: the devils also believe, and tremble.
20. But wilt thou know, O vain man, that faith without works is dead?
21. Was not Abraham our father justified by works, when he had offered Isaac his son upon the altar?
22. Seest thou how faith wrought with his works, and by works was faith made perfect?
24. Ye see then how that by works a man is justified, and not by faith only.
26. For as the body without the spirit is dead, so faith without works is dead also.

From the above scripture we can see that...

- *Faith without works cannot save a man.*
- *Faith cannot survive alone without works.*
- *Faith need works to be alive.*
- *Faith without works is dead.*
- *Faith is likened to a body.*
- *Works is likened to spirit.*
- *Works gives life to faith.*
- *Works is the spirit of faith.*
- *Faith is expressed through works.*
- *Faith without works does not make you any different from the devil.*
- *Faith is made perfect by works.*
- *A man is justified by his works.*
- *Works justifies man.*

The works spoken of by Apostle James is simply the demonstration of faith or taking steps of faith in obedience to God's word, instruction or command. And water baptism is one of such steps we take to demonstrate our faith in Christ.

Jesus Christ in Mark 16:16 shows us the body and spirit relationship of faith and works, how that faith cannot do without works, when He said, *...he that believeth and is baptised shall be saved.*

The same gospel the Lord Jesus preached is the

same gospel, He handed down to the apostles as a commandment. Hear apostle Peter's version of the gospel he received from Jesus.

Acts 2:38. Then Peter said unto them, Repent, and be baptized every one of you in the name of Jesus Christ for the remission of sins, and ye shall receive the gift of the Holy Ghost.
41. Then they that gladly received his word were baptized: and the same day there were added unto them about three thousand souls.

We see that those that received the gospel were baptised, the same day they believed, as commanded by Jesus: preach and baptise those that believe.

One thing we must understand about Peter is that, he is a faithful follower of instructions and commands. Whatever he does is as commanded by the Lord Jesus. It would take God himself to cause Peter to go against any instruction or command of God. Peter would obey the last command unless God himself gives a counter instruction.

Let's look at a practical example. We see that the Lord Jesus at some point had asked the disciples not to preach to the Gentiles.

*Matthew 10:5. These twelve Jesus sent forth, and commanded them, saying, **Go not into the way of the Gentiles, and into any city of the***

Samaritans enter ye not:

6. But go rather to the lost sheep of the house of Israel.

7. And as ye go, preach, saying, The kingdom of heaven is at hand.

And when God needed to send him to a Gentile, He God had to do strange and unusual things for Peter to go against the last command. God had to baptise the Gentiles with the Holy Ghost to prove to Peter that it was his will to save them and to bear witness to the truth that they are ordained for salvation and as such should be baptised. From Peter's teachings we see that Peter had always known and believed that you get baptised in water before you receive the Holy Ghost and for God to baptise anyone with the Holy Ghost before being baptised in water proved to Peter that it was truly God's will for him to preach to the Gentiles at that time for their salvation.

Acts 10:44. While Peter yet spake these words, the Holy Ghost fell on all them which heard the word.

*45. And **they of the circumcision** which believed **were astonished**, as many as came with Peter, because **that on the Gentiles also was poured out the gift of the Holy Ghost.***

46. For they heard them speak with tongues, and magnify God. Then answered Peter,

*47. **Can any man forbid water, that these should not be baptized, which have received the Holy Ghost** as well as we?*

48. And he commanded them to be baptized in the name of the Lord. Then prayed they him to tarry certain days.

Peter always operated the preach, believe, get baptised in water and receive the Holy Spirit ministry. Which is the ministry that was given to him by the Lord Jesus. If it were not so, faithful Peter would not do it. We see therefore that whatever Peter preached and did concerning water baptism, would have been directly commanded by the Lord Jesus Christ.

We see this same kind of mindset in the ministry of Paul the apostle. However, many have misunderstood the words of Paul to say he trivialised the need for water baptism as a fundamental requirement for man's salvation. They take Paul's word that he was not sent to baptise as a downplay of water baptism. Let's take a look at the scripture; I would like you to pay careful attention to every statement in the scripture.

1 Corinthians 1:12. Now this I say, that every one of you saith, I am of Paul; and I of Apollos; and I of Cephas; and I of Christ.

13. Is Christ divided? was Paul crucified for you? or were ye baptized in the name of Paul?

14. I thank God that I baptized none of you,

but Crispus and Gaius;

15. Lest any should say that I had baptized in mine own name.

16. And I baptized also the household of Stephanas: besides, I know not whether I baptized any other.

17. For Christ sent me not to baptize, but to preach the gospel: not with wisdom of words, lest the cross of Christ should be made of none effect.

There was a dispute and division at that time in the church of God at Corinth, where some brethren in the church were choosing the apostles, pastors or ministry they belonged to. Paul had to use water baptism to clear the air, because water baptism was the only mystery that could determine who you belong to. He made it clear to them that he was happy he didn't baptise any of them otherwise they would have used it against him to say they belong to him since he baptised them. Some die hard fans or followers of his could have even claimed he baptised them in his name to prove that they belonged to him.

I thank God that I baptized none of you

Paul wasn't saying that it wasn't necessary to be baptised in water, rather because of the important nature of baptism (which connects or unites you to whom you are baptised in his name), he was using it to make a point to prove that he is not in the ministry to win souls to himself but unto Christ and as such no one should say they are of him or belong to him.

Christ sent me not to baptize, but to preach the gospel:

Paul was not sent to baptise like John the Baptist, rather he was sent to preach the gospel. John the Baptist's ministry was to baptise and as such he had to baptise everyone into his ministry by himself. Paul's ministry was not the ministry of baptism like John's, otherwise he would need to baptise people himself. Paul's ministry was to preach the gospel of Jesus Christ, which means if he preached, those who believe his gospel could be baptised by another person other than him. However, it's important to note that water baptism is a part of the gospel of Jesus Christ or the preaching ministry; it is incorporated into every gospel-preaching ministry. Paul understood this and that is why he had to baptise some people himself and also recommend others to be baptised by his sons. Paul didn't need to baptise people himself, he had many sons like Timothy who could have baptised those Paul preached to. Nevertheless, to lead by example he baptised Crispus, Gaius, Stephanas household and some others he could not remember.

Apostle Paul understood that water baptism was necessary for salvation and for the gift of the Holy Ghost. He recommended the New Testament water baptism to the Ephesian brethren when he discovered that they had not received the Holy Ghost being baptised only with the baptism of John. He had to wait until they were baptised with the New Testament baptism before he could lay his hands on them to receive the Holy Ghost.

> *Acts 19:3. And he said unto them, Unto what then were ye baptized? And they said, Unto John's baptism.*
> *4. Then said Paul, John verily baptized with the baptism of repentance, saying unto the people, that they should believe on him which should come after him, that is, on Christ Jesus.*
> *5. When they heard this, they were baptized in the name of the Lord Jesus.*
> *6. And when Paul had laid his hands upon them, the Holy Ghost came on them; and they spake with tongues, and prophesied.*

We see that Paul also operated the preach, believe, get baptised in water and receive the Holy Spirit kind of ministry which faithful Peter operated.

Paul was fully abreast of the importance of water baptism as a fundamental requirement for salvation, he never downplayed water baptism, as some have ignorantly believed. Paul's ministry may not be to baptise but through his ministry he understood and reveals to us the essence of the mystery of water baptism.

When Paul said we are saved by grace through faith, he understood that our faith in Christ is demonstrated by water baptism. When he talked about works not being necessary for salvation, he wasn't talking about works as an action or demonstration of our faith but works as a human effort of good works that we do or self-righteousness.

The Pauline epistle tries to make us understand that salvation is not by our efforts but by our faith in the finished work of Christ. And of course, we demonstrate our faith in the finished work of Christ through water baptism and we have also seen how that water baptism is powered and made effective by the finished work of Christ (1 Peter 3:21).

Apostle Paul was saying if salvation was by our works, then those of us who were wallowing in sin would never have been saved. Now that is where grace comes in (the free and unmerited favour of God), such that even in our sinfulness yet Christ still died on the cross to save us from our sins (Matthew 1:21). Nevertheless to connect to this grace or to partake of what Christ has done for us, we have to believe in Him and take the necessary steps of faith. Paul was saying we did not get saved because we were righteous at the time we encountered Christ but we got saved despite our sinfulness because we had faith in Christ, which granted us access to the grace of God.

GRACE, FAITH & BAPTISM

Ephesians 2:8. For by grace are ye saved through faith; and that not of yourselves: it is the gift of God:
9. Not of works, lest any man should boast.

Faith in Christ gives us access to the grace of God, however in manifesting that faith that gives you access to the grace of God, there is what to do to demonstrate or give life to your faith in the finished work of Christ, and that which you must do is water baptism.

The scriptural references below will help our understanding.

Titus 3:3. For we ourselves also were sometimes foolish, disobedient, deceived, serving divers lusts and pleasures, living in malice and envy, hateful, and hating one another.
4. But after that the kindness and love of God our Saviour toward man appeared,
*5. Not by works of righteousness which we have done, but according to his mercy **he saved us, by the washing of regeneration, and renewing of the Holy Ghost;***
6. Which he shed on us abundantly through Jesus Christ our Saviour;
7. That being justified by his grace, we should

be made heirs according to the hope of eternal life.

We see that we are not saved by the works of righteousness that we have done but by the washing of regeneration (water baptism) and the renewing of the Spirit. Exactly what the Lord Jesus said would get us born again in John three verse five: water and Spirit.

The New International Version puts Titus 3:5 this way...

Titus 3:5 (NIV). He saved us not because of the righteous things we had done, but because of his mercy. He saved us through the washing of new birth and renewal by the Holy Spirit.

"He saved us through the washing of new birth and renewal by the Holy Spirit."

We see that this is more like a paraphrase of the born of water and of the Spirit spoken of by Jesus in John three verse five. Note that this was apostle Paul speaking about water baptism as a medium for salvation, also note that this same Paul who said we are saved by grace through faith, spoke and revealed more about water baptism than the rest of the apostles.

Paul was trying to make us understand that while we were still enjoying our sinful lives, living in disobedience unto God, God sent His Son to die for us to save us. He wasn't saying that because we are saved by grace, we should do nothing or not get baptised. He was trying to disabuse our minds from thinking we can **earn** salvation.

Ephesians 2:1. And you hath he quickened, who were dead in trespasses and sins;

2. Wherein in time past ye walked according to the course of this world, according to the prince of the power of the air, the spirit that now worketh in the children of disobedience:

3. Among whom also we all had our conversation in times past in the lusts of our flesh, fulfilling the desires of the flesh and of the mind; and were by nature the children of wrath, even as others.

4. But God, who is rich in mercy, for his great love wherewith he loved us,

5. Even when we were dead in sins, hath quickened us together with Christ, (by grace ye are saved;)

6. And hath raised us up together, and made us sit together in heavenly places in Christ Jesus:

7. That in the ages to come he might shew the exceeding riches of his grace in his kindness toward us through Christ Jesus.

8. For by grace are ye saved through faith; and that not of yourselves: it is the gift of God:

9. Not of works, lest any man should boast.

We cannot earn salvation neither can we earn grace. Paul is saying we cannot boost that we were saved because we were living righteous but rather because we have faith in Jesus and His finished work on the cross. And do not forget that whenever we see faith, water baptism must follow to make this faith dynamic and alive.

Romans 5:1. Therefore being justified by faith, we have peace with God through our Lord Jesus Christ:
2. By whom also we have access by faith into this grace wherein we stand, and rejoice in hope of the glory of God.
8. But God commendeth his love toward us, in that, while we were yet sinners, Christ died for us.

Christ died for us while we were yet sinners to grant us access to grace, now that is a gift we do not deserve but to gain access to this gift of grace we need to believe in Christ. Our faith in Christ grants us access to the grace of God, and faith is not just a mental perception but also a practical act of obedience to the truth.

We must understand that we don't move God by our mental faith, rather we move God by taking steps of faith. Our faith cannot change God's word because it is through the word of God that we receive faith, *for faith comes by hearing the word of God.* This word of God could come as an instruction or as a command, which requires our obedience. We experience faith when we receive God's instruction and we demonstrate faith when we take steps to obey this instructions and command.

> *Romans 3:22. Even the righteousness of God which is by faith of Jesus Christ unto all and upon all them that believe: for there is no difference:*
> *24. Being justified freely by his grace through the redemption that is in Christ Jesus:*
> *28. Therefore we conclude that a man is justified by faith without the deeds of the law.*

We are justified because we believe in Jesus not because we keep the laws. We receive the righteousness of God through faith in the redemption that is in Jesus Christ. Nevertheless, we demonstrate our faith in Christ by being buried with him in baptism.

GRACE AS A GIFT

You know many people believe that grace is a free gift of God (a gift we do not receive by our own efforts) and as such we don't need to do anything to receive this gift of grace. Now, let's take a look at grace as a gift to help us understand what to do to enjoy the gift of grace.

Grace is a gift as seen in Ephesians 2:8 and Ephesians 3:7.

Ephesians 2:8. For by grace are ye saved through faith; and that not of yourselves: it is the gift of God:

And like every gift, to receive grace there must be an exchange from the giver of grace to the receiver of grace. A gift is of no value to whoever it is intended as long as it remains in the hand of the giver. For a gift to be a blessing to anyone, they must have received it from whoever is giving it. It's important to note that water baptism unites us with Christ (the giver of grace) in other to receive the gift of grace.

The wise preacher, king Solomon tells us that, the fact that we are able to eat, drink and enjoy what we labour for, is a gift of God.

Ecclesiastes 3:13. And also that every man should eat and drink, and enjoy the good of all his labour, it is the gift of God.

Ecclesiastes 5:19. Every man also to whom God hath given riches and wealth, and hath given him power to eat thereof, and to take his portion, and to rejoice in his labour; this is the gift of God.

Now, though this is a gift of God, yet if we choose not to do anything (not to eat what we have laboured for or not to labour at all), there is no way we would enjoy this gift of enjoying what we labour for.

The gift of grace is like the gift of enjoying our labour but we have to labour or do something to enjoy this gift. If we decide to do nothing (though this gift is readily available) we would not be able to enjoy this free gift of God. We take gifts by doing something, every gift that is given to us demands that we take it. We don't take gifts by doing nothing; neither do we take the gift of grace by doing nothing. Baptism is what we must do to take or receive grace. Yes! We take grace at baptism; we take the grace that Jesus came to give to us at baptism. Baptism is the meeting point where grace is exchanged from the giver to the receiver.

That grace is a gift does not mean that we should do nothing to receive it. Think about it, eternal life is a gift (Romans 6:23) but you have to believe in Jesus to receive it (John 3:16). The Holy Ghost is a gift but you have to repent and be baptised to receive it (Acts 2:38). In the same vain grace is a gift but you have to be baptised into Christ to receive it.

*Acts 2:38. Then Peter said unto them, **Repent, and be baptized** every one of you in the name of Jesus Christ for the remission of sins, **and ye*** *shall receive the gift of the Holy Ghost.*

Let's take a look at another illustration.

Now, let's assume your teacher phoned you and said, "Hey! I have a gift for you. I would like to give it to you but you must meet me at school to pick it up."

The question now is...

Is your teacher offering you a free gift? Yes!

Did you earn this gift? No!

Will going to your school to get the gift mean that you have earned this gift? No! It is still a gift. But you must take certain steps in order to receive this gift. If you refuse to take those steps, you will receive nothing.

Receiving God's free gift of salvation and eternal life involves the same principle. You have not earned it, but you have to do what God the giver of the gift instructs if you desire to receive it.

WATER BAPTISM AND THE ELECTION OF GRACE

You know, some anointed men of God think that because they can perform great miracles, exercise dominion over sicknesses and evil spirits, they do not need water baptism. But they miss out on the truth.

From scriptures we see that the name of Jesus Christ is a very powerful name and that any man who engages the name of Jesus in faith can cast out devils in the name even without being a follower of Jesus.

Luke 9:49. And John answered and said, Master, we saw one casting out devils in thy name; and we forbad him, because he followeth not with us.
*50. And Jesus said unto him, **Forbid him not**: for he that is not against us is for us.*

Jesus does not forbid people from using His name to cast out devils. So anyone can use His name to cast out devils when they use it with faith. Therefore, that you are casting out devils is not a proof that you are a child of God, a follower of Christ or a candidate of heaven.

Hear what the Lord Jesus himself said...

Matthew 7:21. Not every one that saith unto me, Lord, Lord, shall enter into the kingdom of heaven; but he that doeth the will of my Father which is in heaven.
22. Many will say to me in that day, Lord, Lord, have we not prophesied in thy name? and in thy name have cast out devils? and in thy name done many wonderful works?
23. And then will I profess unto them, I never knew you: depart from me, ye that work iniquity.

I believe water baptism is one of the will of the Father that we must do because it is a command from

God through Jesus. We see that not doing the will of God by rejecting water baptism can hinder us from entering heaven.

Preaching the gospel, casting out devils, healing the sick and doing many wonderful works is not a proof that we are in Christ, there are many non-Christians and Satanist's who can do miracles. We see miracles in Buddhism, yoga etc but that does not mean they are of God or in Christ. The ancient Egyptian magicians also performed the same miracles that Moses did but that didn't mean they were of God. That you do signs and wonders without getting baptised doesn't mean you are in Christ.

No wonder the Lord Jesus said to His disciples, *don't rejoice because the spirits are subject unto you; but rather rejoice, because your names are written in heaven* (Luke 10:20). And we have seen that doing God's will is what grants us access to heaven and its registry. It would be unfortunate to cast out devils, have the spirits under our subjection and yet not have our names in heavens registry. Water baptism I believe grants us access to heaven's registry, to have our names written with the ink of the blood of the Lamb in the Lamb's book of life.

My father in the Lord, Bishop David Oyedepo, (a prophet whom I respect and believe in so much) made a profound statement that encouraged me in the course of writing this chapter of this book. He said he got baptised in water as a guest minister at a conference when a certain preacher ministered about water baptism. He said he was baptised as an infant on the 8th day after his birth but was excited that Jesus had not come before he got this opportunity to know the truth about water baptism and get baptised again. He made these statements at a leadership empowerment summit on the 5th of January 2019 (which happened to be my birthday), where I was drinking from the rivers of living waters flowing from him. Perhaps he was pastoring a great church and doing great miracles for God at that time but when he got the knowledge of the importance of water baptism, he did not hesitate to get baptised in water immediately. This I believe is a worthy example to follow.

From the teaching of the apostles and other scriptural references, I have always believed that water baptism precedes the Holy Ghost baptism. And as such at some point in the course of writing this chapter of this book, I was bothered with the question in my heart of whether all anointed ministers were baptised in water before they were able to do all the great things they could do. When I read in the book "Living a Life of fire" by Reinhard Bonnke how that he got baptised in the Holy Ghost at age 11 before getting baptised in water, I began to wonder if water baptism was not necessary for the empowerment of the Holy Ghost as taught by the apostles. But then comparing these real life experiences with scriptural experiences, I realise that God makes exceptions to break this protocol, in other to clear off barriers of unworthiness on the path of the called and to bear witness that it was His will to save them. This is seen in the story of Cornelius and his household in acts chapter ten and the story of Reinhard Bonnke, and perhaps many other anointed men/women of God.

Like Cornelius, Bonnke's parent had thought he was not ready or worthy for the baptism of the Holy Ghost. In Bonnke's book, after he was filled with the Holy Spirit He said...

"Every day that followed, I begged my parents to allow me to follow the Lord in water baptism. I was eager to identify completely with Jesus after being filled with the Spirit. Mother's response was, "If the Lord was willing to baptize him in the Holy Spirit at such a young age, how can we deny him water baptism."

I see that even though water baptism precedes the Holy Ghost baptism, yet God can choose to make an exception for some people, (for those called according to the election of grace). God can choose to baptise men with the Holy Ghost without them first being baptised in water. However, that does not change the fact that we still need to be baptised in water. The baptism of the Holy Ghost should rather stir us up to be baptised in water without delay. I see this truth in the story of Reinhard Bonnke and in the story of Cornelius.

Acts 10:47. Can any man forbid water, that these should not be baptized, which have received the Holy Ghost as well as we?
48. And he commanded them to be baptized in the name of the Lord. Then prayed they him to tarry certain days.

The baptism of the Holy Ghost on those who were not baptised in water always facilitated their being baptised in water.

Beloved, are you in this category of men that God makes exceptions for? You must be very special to God, called according to the election of grace. Please make God's exception in your life by the election of grace count by identifying with the Lord in water baptism.

FINAL WORDS FROM THE SAVIOUR

Let's read the final words of the Lord Jesus, the Author and Finisher of our faith, after His death and resurrection when He gave the great commission.

Matthew 28:18. And Jesus came and spake unto them, saying, All power is given unto me in heaven and in earth.
19. Go ye therefore, and teach all nations, ***baptizing them*** *in the name of the Father, and of the Son, and of the Holy Ghost:*

*20. **Teaching them to observe all things whatsoever I have commanded you**: and, lo, I am with you alway, even unto the end of the world. Amen.*

Mark 16:15. And he said unto them, Go ye into all the world, and preach the gospel to every creature.
*16. He that believeth and is **baptized** shall be saved; but he that believeth not shall be damned.*

Note that when the Lord Jesus gave the command of the great commission He had already resurrected from the dead and grace was available at that time. Yet He emphasised the need for water baptism. The fact that none of the eyewitnesses missed water baptism in their account of the great commission reflects the importance of water baptism.

Note also that in apostle Matthew's account of the great commission, faith was not captured, this I believe is because he saw baptism as a demonstration of faith and as such there can't be baptism without first believing. What Philip said to the Ethiopian eunuch validates this truth.

Acts 8:35. Then Philip opened his mouth, and began at the same scripture, and preached unto him Jesus.

36. And as they went on their way, they came unto a certain water: and the eunuch said, See, here is water; what doth hinder me to be baptized?

*37. And Philip said, **If thou believest with all thine heart, thou mayest**. And he answered and said, I believe that Jesus Christ is the Son of God.*

Note that Philip preached Jesus, then the eunuch believed and then got baptised, just inline with what was instructed in the great commission as captured by apostle Mark. If Philip had not preached water baptism to the eunuch, as commanded by Jesus, *believe and be baptised*, the eunuch wouldn't have seen the need to be baptised. Note that it was recorded that Philip preached Jesus to the eunuch but the eunuch's response to the preaching was to be baptised into Christ. If Philip had not preached water baptism as he preached Jesus to the eunuch, the eunuch would not see the need to get baptised. This goes to show that **you can't preach Jesus without preaching water baptism**. Note that what Philip preached was among the early gospels that were preached by the disciples of Jesus as led by the Holy Ghost. Water baptism is a part of the gospel of Jesus Christ that we must preach as pastors and church leaders. As church leaders if we are not preaching water baptism as an integral part of the great commission (or as an integral part of the gospel of Jesus Christ for the salvation of men), we are not being faithful in the great commission, we are ignorantly hindering many from being saved, and ignorance as we know is not an excuse before God, it is one reason many people of God are destroyed (Hosea 4:6).

Note what the Lord Jesus said when He gave the great commission. He said GO, TEACH and BAPTIZE and He said *"Teaching them to observe all things whatsoever I have commanded you:"* We must teach men to observe what Jesus has commanded us and water baptism is not just one of such commandments commanded by Jesus but it is also one of the most important of these commandments. **Water baptism is one of the commandments of Jesus that we must teach men to observe.**

Our responsibility in the great commission is to teach or preach the gospel of Jesus Christ and baptise those who believe this gospel. Unfortunately many church leaders today are not teaching men to observe water baptism, these men are not preaching the gospel of Jesus Christ but the lie of the devil. Any gospel that removes or downplays water baptism is of the devil.

On a final note, to fulfil the great commission, **we cannot preach the gospel of Jesus Christ without preaching water baptism and teaching men to observe it.**

8

Is there place for Rebaptism?

You know many Christians have been doctrinally made to believe that water baptism should only be done once and the popular scripture they use to drive this home is Ephesians 4:5 which talks about one baptism.

Ephesians 4:4. There is one body, and one Spirit, even as ye are called in one hope of your calling;

5. One Lord, one faith, one baptism,

6. One God and Father of all, who is above all, and through all, and in you all.

The bible says there is one baptism, but that doesn't mean that baptism should be done once. It simply means there is only one true baptism. We have seen from scriptures that there are many water baptisms, baptism of John, Old Testament baptism and many other baptisms (associated with other contemporary religions), but the truth remains that there is only one true baptism, which is the baptism of Jesus Christ.

What the scripture above is saying is that there are many baptisms but there is only one true baptism, which is the baptism of Jesus Christ. The same scripture that says there is one baptism also says there is one body, one Spirit, one faith, one God, one Lord, one Father but you and I know that there are many bodies, many spirits, many faiths (eg. Islam, Buddhism, Hinduism, Judaism etc), many gods, many lords and many fathers. What the scripture is simply implying is that there could be many spirits but there is only one true Holy Spirit, there could be many bodies but is one true body of Christ, there could be many faiths but there is one true faith (which is the Christian Faith), there could be many gods but there is one Almighty God, there could be many lords but there is one true Lord (the Lord of lords), there could be many fathers but there is one true Father, the Heavenly Father, the Father of all.

Having established therefore that the above scripture on one baptism refers to the one true baptism of Jesus Christ by immersion, we must ensure that we get baptised with the one true baptism. This implies that if we have been baptised wrongly either by aspersion, affusion, or in another name other than the name of

Jesus Christ or the Godhead, we must get rebaptised **by immersion** in the name of the Father and of the Son and of the Holy Spirit.

Let's look at an example in the bible where believers were rebaptised when they got to know the truth about water baptism.

Acts 19:2. He said unto them, Have ye received the Holy Ghost since ye believed? And they said unto him, We have not so much as heard whether there be any Holy Ghost.

*3. And he said unto them, **Unto what then were ye baptized? And they said, Unto John's baptism.***

4. Then said Paul, John verily baptized with the baptism of repentance, saying unto the people, that they should believe on him which should come after him, that is, on Christ Jesus.

*5. **When they heard this, they were baptized in the name of the Lord Jesus.***

6. And when Paul had laid his hands upon them, the Holy Ghost came on them; and they spake with tongues, and prophesied.

Did you see rebaptism in verse five above?

The Ephesian brethren did not hesitate to get baptised again when they heard the truth. Perhaps you have been baptised wrongly in the past, now that you have heard the truth about water baptism, please do not hesitate to get rebaptized, do not hesitate to get it right with the mystery of water baptism.

You know, many believers get worried about getting baptised a second time, but what we should worry more about should be about getting it right. I believe God will not punish anyone for getting baptised many times just to ensure that they get it right, just as God will not punish a backslider for rededicating his life to Jesus Christ many times.

We must let it sink into our subconscious that water baptism is not a one-off ordinance but an ordinance that must be done right. Just as there is room for a backslider to rededicate his life to God, there is also room for rebaptism.

Water baptism is not attributed to any church denomination, it is simply an ordinance that every Christian must observe to do. As such we must understand that when we are baptised, we are not baptised into a church but into Christ. We may be baptised in a church or but we are not baptised into that church, otherwise the dispute and division that arose with Paul and other church leaders as recorded in first Corinthians one verse twelve will overwhelm our hearts. In other words, don't get too attached to a church because you were baptised there.

Don't leave your destiny to chance based on what you have been told. Discover the truth for yourself and get it right. Through this book I believe you now know the truth.

Conclusion

Water baptism is a spiritual ordinance given by God for the spiritual rebirth of His children. This ordinance is fundamental for the spiritual rebirth and growth of every believer.

I see water baptism by immersion as an ancient landmark that must not be removed, neither it nor its foundation.

Water baptism as an ancient landmark marks a turning point in the life of a believer: from darkness into light, from carnal to spiritual, from earthly to heavenly, from the kingdom of this world into the kingdom of the Lord Jesus.

This ordinance does not only represent a transition point in the life of a believer but it also determines the spiritual development of the believer. The need to get this mystery right can therefore not be overemphasised, as believers need it for their spiritual growth and development.

Therefore, if you have not been baptised by immersion in the name of Jesus Christ, why tarry ye?

Make haste and get baptised today.

Be washed and made brand new.

Start a brand new life in Christ.

And remain ever blessed in the Lord.

HOW TO APPROACH THE WATER WHEN BEING BAPTISED

We must not enter the water casually to be baptised, it is an important spiritual mystery and demands a spiritual approach. Below are some scriptural approaches or things to do while being baptised.

1. Enter the water confessing your sins.

*Mark 1:5. And there went out unto him all the land of Judaea, and they of Jerusalem, and **were all baptized** of him in the river of Jordan, **confessing their sins**.*

We must enter the water confessing our sins. We may not confess it openly for others to hear but let God hear our confession. Confess your sins before God and tell Him how sorry and repentant you are. Jesus didn't have any sin, so He had no sin to confess. He rather entered the water praying.

2. Enter the water prayerfully.

*Luke 3:21. Now when all the people were baptized, it came to pass, that **Jesus also being baptized, and praying, the heaven was opened**,*

We must enter the water praying. We must ask what we want God to do for us, *for he that asks receives*. We could pray for God to open our heaven, baptise us with the Holy Spirit, reveal Himself to us, reveal to us His purpose for our life, spiritually circumcise us, empower us with every grace we need to fulfil purpose, bring to pass in our life speedily every benefit of water baptism. Perhaps what Jesus was praying about when He entered the water was what we saw manifest at His baptism.

3. **Enter the water thirsting and craving for the Holy Spirit and asking God to fill you with the Holy Spirit.**

*Psalm 63:1. O God, thou art my God; early will I seek thee: **my soul thirsteth for thee**, my flesh longeth for thee in a dry and thirsty land, where no water is;*
*2. **To see thy power and thy glory**, so as I have seen thee in the sanctuary.*

The Holy Spirit is the power of God and to see the power and the glory of God as seen above, we must thirst for God the Holy Spirit.
Thirst is the currency for receiving the Holy Spirit.
God is willing to give His Spirit to us freely but we must thirst for Him, if we must receive Him.

*Isaiah 55:1. Ho, **every one that thirsteth, come ye to the waters,** and he that hath no money; come ye, buy, and eat; yea, come, buy wine and milk **without money and without price.***

We see from scriptures that the Holy Spirit is often referred to as water. This reference helps us to understand the importance of thirsting for the Holy Spirit. By understanding how it feels to thirst for water, we understand better what it means to thirst for the Holy Spirit. A man who is thirsty of water will not stop seeking water until he finds it and his thirst is quenched, in the same manner a man thirsty of the Holy Spirit will keep seeking and asking God for it until he is filled. Until we are filled with the Holy Spirit with visible scriptural proofs we must not stop asking God for the infilling of the Holy Spirit.

*Isaiah 44:3. For **I will pour water upon him that is thirsty**, and floods upon the dry ground: **I will pour my spirit upon thy seed**, and my blessing upon thine offspring:*

*John 7:37. In the last day, that great day of the feast, Jesus stood and cried, saying, **If any man thirst, let him come unto me, and drink.***
*38. He that believeth on me, as the scripture hath said, **out of his belly shall flow rivers of living water.***
*39. (**But this spake he of the Spirit**, which they that believe on him should receive: for the Holy Ghost was not yet given; because that Jesus was not yet glorified.)*

We see the Lord Jesus in the scripture above referring

to the Holy Spirit as living water.

God is willing to give the Holy Spirit to every believer that asks for it but the condition is that we must thirst for it. God gives us the Holy Spirit as willingly as a father gives bread to His hungry children.

Luke 11:13. If ye then, being evil, know how to give good gifts unto your children: **how much more shall your heavenly Father give the Holy Spirit to them that ask him?**

The Lord Jesus reveals to us in many scriptures how that to be filled with the Holy Spirit we must hunger and thirst for Him. In the book of Matthew chapter five verse six, the Lord Jesus reveals to us that *those who hunger and thirst for the Holy Spirit shall be filled.*

Matthew 5:6. Blessed are they which do hunger and thirst after righteousness: for they shall be filled.

This statement was made in reference to the Holy Spirit, the Holy Spirit is the spirit of righteousness or holiness. Instead of calling Him the Holy Spirit, you can still call Him the Holiness Spirit or the Spirit of Holiness. We see this truth validated by apostle Paul in his teachings when he said the Lord **Jesus is declared to be the Son of God with power, according to the spirit of holiness (Romans 1:4)**

It is important therefore to thirst for the Holy Spirit if we must be filled. *For Blessed are they which do hunger and thirst after the Holy Spirit: for they shall be filled.*

4. See the water as God's tool for your spiritual circumcision.

*Colossians 2:11. In whom also ye are circumcised with **the circumcision made without hands,** in putting off the body of the sins of the flesh by **the circumcision of Christ:***
12. Buried with him in baptism, wherein also ye are risen with him through the faith of the operation of God, who hath raised him from the dead.

God has a tool for everything; the water in which we are being baptised is God's tool for the sanctification, purification and spiritual circumcision of our body. We must see the water in this light so that we don't make light of it. Any water meant for baptism is not ordinary water. As soon as that water has been separated for baptism it becomes empowered by Jesus for the purpose of the spiritual rebirth of a Christian and ceases to become ordinary water.

5. **See the water as the mixture of water and the blood of Jesus.**

*John 19:34. But one of the soldiers with a spear pierced his side, and forthwith came there out **blood and water.***

*1 John 5:6. **This is he that came by water and blood, even Jesus Christ;** not by water only, but by water and blood. And it is the Spirit that beareth witness, because the Spirit is truth.*

The blood of Jesus Christ makes water baptism an effective tool for man's salvation; we must see it as such. We must see the water as the mixture of the blood and water that came out of Jesus for the purification of our body. The blood of Jesus purifies and makes the water for our baptism pure. The water might look murky to the natural eyes (which is common with river, in cases where a river is being used), but we must see it that because the water is to be used for baptism, the blood of Jesus has made it pure even though it may look murky to the eyes.

6. **See that Jesus is baptising you spiritually, even though man is baptising you physically.**

While men baptise here physically, Jesus is also busy baptising us spiritually. The bible tells us that while we are being baptised here on earth, Jesus is there circumcision us spiritually. While we are baptised physically, spiritually Jesus is circumcising us, with a circumcision not made by human hands but by the hands of Jesus.

Colossians 2:11. In whom also ye are circumcised with the circumcision made without hands, in putting off the body of the sins of the flesh by **the circumcision of Christ:**

Men are often an extension of God's hand for the manifestation of His great acts.
Note that Samuel anointed David, but when God was speaking about that same anointing, He said He was the one that anointed David with the oil.

1 Samuel 16:13. Then **Samuel took the horn of oil, and anointed him** *in the midst of his brethren: and the Spirit of the LORD came upon David from that day forward. So Samuel rose up, and went to Ramah.*

Psalm 89:20. **I have found David** *my servant;* **with my holy oil have I anointed him:**

Samuel may have anointed David physically but spiritually God was the one anointing David. In the same vain, man may be baptising you physically but spiritually Jesus is the one baptising you.

ABOUT THE AUTHOR

Christopher Ogan is an anointed scribe in the hand of the Almighty God.

The LORD has put His words in his mouth to be a blessing to mankind.

He was born as Christ-Bearer, with a mission to bear the gospel of Jesus Christ to the world.

He is passionate about God, His word and His kingdom.

He is married to his beloved wife Esther and are blessed with children.